Mad About

Pastas & Cheese

Other books in this series:

MAD ABOUT FISH & SEAFOOD
MAD ABOUT MUSHROOMS
MAD ABOUT RASPBERRIES & STRAWBERRIES

Other books by Jacqueline Hériteau:

GROW IT, COOK IT
A FEAST OF SOUPS
ORIENTAL COOKING THE FAST WOK WAY
HOW TO GROW AND CAN IT

Mad About

Pastas &
Cheese

by Jacqueline Hériteau

illustrations by Woodleigh Hubbard

A GD/Perigee Book

Perigee Books
are published by
The Putnam Publishing Group
200 Madison Avenue
New York, New York 10016

Typeset by International Computaprint Corp.

Library of Congress Cataloging in Publication Data

Hériteau, Jacqueline.
    Mad about pastas & cheese.

    "A GD/Perigee book."
    Includes index.
    1. Cookery (Macaroni) 2. Cookery (Cheese)
I. Title.   II. Title: Mad about pastas and cheese.
TX809.M17H47   1984   641.8'22   83-23748
ISBN 0-399-50992-5

First Perigee printing, 1984

Printed in the United States of America

1 2 3 4 5 6 7 8 9

Cover recipes include:
(front) Fettuccini and Salsa Bianca, page 12, garnished with ripe
olives; homemade pastas, page 11;
(back) Tortellini al Pesto with Mozzarella, page 20; Lasagna with
Red Clam Sauce, page 26; Chocolate Pasta, Brandy and Cream,
page 61; Café Espresso, page 63.
Flowers designed by Hunter Flowers, Park Avenue, New York City.

CONTENTS

Food makes happiness. The MAD ABOUT books are about the fun of cooking your favorite foods—the joy of sharing new and interesting foodscapes, the satisfaction of binging—tastefully. The philosophy of the series is that when you start with ingredients that you love—pastas and cheeses, fresh herbs, vegetables, butter, eggs—and the very best recipe, you and those who dine at your table are bound to have a wonderful time. If you cook to relax as well as to eat but don't have hours a day to shop and hover over the stove, you'll truly appreciate the MAD ABOUT approach to cuisine. You will find valuable general information on the next few pages.

Pasta with herbs, vegetables, cheeses 12: from FETTUCCINE WITH SALSA BIANCA and PASTA AL PESTO to SPINACH AND CHEESE RAVIOLI.

Sea sauces 24: from SPAGHETTINI WITH WHITE CLAM SAUCE to FETTUCCINE WITH LOBSTER SAUCE, LASAGNA WITH RED CLAM SAUCE, and SPAGHETTINI WITH MARINARA SAUCE.

Meat and Chicken Sauces 34: from LASAGNA WITH BOLOGNESE SAUCE to SPAGHETTI WITH HAMBURGERS LAFAYETTE.

Salads and starters 44: from SALAD (AND) DRESSING MAISON and GREEK SALAD WITH FETA CHEESE to TORTIGLIONI VINAIGRETTE WITH ARTICHOKES.

The pasta dinner 54: from ANTIPASTO PLATTER and GARLIC BREAD to CHOCOLATE PASTA WITH BRANDY AND CREAM, RUM CAKE, and CAFÉ ESPRESSO.

Recipe list 64.

SO LIGHT! SO EASY!

Do you cook to relax and to have fun? Does your family eat for the joy of it, not just to fill up? If so, you'll be mad for these pasta and cheese dinners because they are fun and for the wicked, awful reason that with little effort and time, you can turn out pastas you enjoy as much as those that are served in fine Italian restaurants. You'll love the applause that greets White Clam Sauce, Pesto, Pasta Marinara, and Egg Drop Soup you make at home. The key to pasta happiness is simple—the very best recipes and fine, fresh ingredients. Is pasta cookery expensive? Do we wear our pastas around our waists? No, because small portions of really good pasta and cheese are satisfying.

WHAT TO SERVE WITH PASTA MEALS

I first had pasta meals years ago on an Italian liner traveling from Cannes to Montreal. In Italian tradition, the pasta was the second course of a four-course dinner, positioned between appetizer (antipasto) and entrée. With the entrée came a tossed salad, and the fourth course was a dessert cheese, with or without fruit, or a sweet. Then, café espresso. Much like a French meal. Not everyone cares to remember that haute cuisine was introduced to the French court by an Italian princess, Caterina de Medici.

Sometime, try a six-course Italian dinner: Antipasto Platter, page 54; Egg Drop Soup, page 56; pasta of your choice; entrée, such as Veal Scaloppine, page 58; salad of tossed greens, page 44; plate of Italian cheeses; café espresso, page 63. Make the centerpiece a combination of flowers—geraniums, carnations, for instance, and fresh foods, asparagus, artichokes, cherries, figs, grapes. Play classical guitar music. Light candles. Ummmm! But for everyday fare, serve pasta as a main course in a light, light, light meal. Choose a meatless pasta from those on pages 12 through 23. Serve with it a salad, either of tossed greens, or a substantial one like the Greek Salad with Feta Cheese, or the Tomato Brie Platter with basil sauce, pages 48–49. Offer bread with butter, hot, crusty Italian flutes or big round peasant loaves—so not one drop of the wonderful sauce will be left, wasted, on the plate. Follow with a sweet, or finger fruits. If you serve a starter course, think of vegetable platters either à la vinaigrette, or such as artichokes with lemon-butter sauce or clams on the half shell, or fragrant wedges of ripe cantaloupe wrapped in paper-thin, elegant prosciutto.

WHAT TO DRINK WITH PASTA MEALS

In Italy, as in France, wine is taken with meals. In recent years, many Italian wines have become popular here. In addition to red and white Chiantis (which are regional *vins ordinaires*), there are light, lovely Soaves from Venice: Valpolicellas; Bardolinos; Orvieto and Frascati from Lazio, and fruity bubblies, such as Asti Spumante.

If you serve wine, choose red to offer with meaty, richly flavored dishes such as Fettuccine Cacciatore, page 41, and white to serve with delicate pasta sauces such as White Clam Sauce, page 24. If you offer drinks before dinner, offer a light aperitif such as an Italian vermouth. If you do not serve alcoholic beverages, Perrier with lime wedges, club soda with lemon twists, or a light ginger ale go well. If you cook without wines, the few dishes here flavored with wine may be made by substituting a wine vinegar diluted with water to suit your palate. Or try cranberry juice.

Coffee ends the pasta meal in a good restaurant. It is generally made from a dark, rich roast sold as French roast in New York. Proportions for one cup are 4 to 5 ounces of boiling water dripped through a filter holding 2 tablespoons of coffee beans that have been ground fine. Add sugar, no milk or cream.

SUCCESS EVERY TIME

Making wonderful pastas is easy when you understand the timing. Many people think the sauces must cook forever. They needn't. Most cook just for minutes! The other thing is not to drown your pastas in Parmesan cheese and the product of the ubiquitous pepper mill. The current practice of dousing every pasta sauce, no matter how delicate and exquisitely balanced, with sneezy hot pepper is like hiding Oriental cookery behind MSG.

Cook pastas in lots of boiling water—4 to 5 quarts at least. Cover the pot to bring it rapidly to a boil, and add 2 tablespoons of salt. I add twice as much salt and a little oil when the pasta is intended for a salad or lasagna dishes, and rinse

the cooked pasta in cold water as soon as it is drained, to help the strands stay separate. Cook pasta uncovered, or it boils over. Take it from the boiling water before it is entirely tender—30 seconds for tiny, just-made pastas; up to 15 minutes for commercial types. *Al dente* is the phrase that describes this state: it means "resistant to the tooth." Just how resistant your tooth wants the pasta to be is up to you, but if you cook it completely tender, its own heat will cook it to mush before you can eat it.

About the difference in cooking times between commercial brands and just-made pastas: pasta made in your kitchen and dried only a few hours will cook in 3 to 5 minutes. Pasta sold as "fresh" in a specialty shop will require a few moments more than that. Pasta sold as "fresh" in a supermarket probably is older, and will take more cooking yet. Test for doneness often, beginning several minutes before the pasta is due to be done.

The instant your pasta is drained, toss it with its sauce. Its heat has some role to play in finishing most sauces, for instance, Pesto, page 13, and Spaghettini Carbonara, page 38. Typically, its heat melts the cheese. The sauce is also crucial to the just-drained pasta. Unless the pasta gets into the sauce at once, it may become a stuck-together mess. Pasta cooking is easy, but it has a rhythm, and at the end, it moves quickly.

To sum up: make the sauce, and cook the pasta while the sauce is finishing. Pour the sauce into a warmed serving dish, drain the pasta, toss it with the sauce at once, and serve immediately, with or without more Parmesan and the pepper mill. To decide whether a dish needs more of either, put a little pasta in a bowl and add Parmesan, then add pepper. If you find that more cheese significantly improves the dish, then add it. Tasting is what makes the difference between a dish that is perfect to your taste and one not quite.

Equipment for cooking pastas consists mainly of a 4- or 5-quart kettle, an enameled or other baking dish for serving the pastas, and a lasagna pan or rectangular baking dish 13 to 15 inches long by 8 to 9 inches wide. The big kettle is a must because pasta needs room to boil around in or it will be partially uncooked when finished, and floury. Boiling with salt and water darkens my kettle, which is aluminum, so now and then to shine it up I fill it with water, add 5 tablespoons of cream of tartar, and boil for 10 minutes.

THE PASTA LARDER

Olive oil: Essential to many pasta sauces that are made with and without butter. The olive flavor is unique, and the better the oil, the better the sauce. De Laurentiis sells his gorgeous green-gold virgin oil for almost $20 a liter (a bit more than a quart), and it is wonderful. But $6 buys a fine olive oil at a Pasta & Cheese Shop, and there are probably good, moderately priced olive oils at your grocer's. Be sure to select a fast-selling brand: Parked on a shelf, it can become rancid and ruin everything.

Butter: The freshest butter makes the best sauce. We make our own by beating heavy cream for 10 minutes till it turns from whipped cream to butterfat. Next step is to press gently into a sieve, then rinse in cold water to clear away the milky residue (save the milk!). Adding 1/4 teaspoon salt before beating produces salt butter; omitting it produces sweet.

Heavy cream: To make butter; to enrich sauces.

Garlic: Essential. Pick plump, firm heads with huge cloves (easier to peel). Mince or crush according to recipe instructions; it makes a difference. To peel easily, whack the clove first with your hand or a heavy knife.

Green onions: Easy to handle and suitable for most recipes. For a substitute for shallots, combine green onions and a sliver of garlic. A green onion "trimmed" means outer skin removed and the green cut to 1 inch.

Pepper mill and black peppercorns: Really essential to zip up creamy sauces and smooth pastas. Store fresh black pepper in a closed container.

Tomato paste: Buy imported in a tube, to pep up pale sauces. Also keep on hand paste in 6-ounce cans for more generous use.

Tomatoes in tomato puree: Better than most fresh tomatoes, unless the tomatoes have been garden ripened, for making pasta sauces.

Cheese: Parmesan is the one most often called for in pasta recipes. Parmesan-Reggiano is the best, but you will be offered "grana" types suitable for grating that are less exquisite. A good grating Parmesan is fine; it doesn't have to be of eating quality. Pecorino Romano is the best Romano. Whatever you do, don't buy grated cheese.

Anchovies: Flat, packed in oil—essential for a number of sauces.

Herbs, fresh and dried: Grow basil in sunny windows, and thyme, oregano, rosemary, tarragon, fennel, and parsley as well. They are essential, too.

ABOUT PASTA SHAPES

Spaghetti

Spaghettini

Fettuccini

Tagliatelle

Capellini

Pappardelle

Lasagna
(½ size)

Pasta comes in an array of shapes and names that vary according to the region of their origin. The basic dough is made of flour and eggs, rolled out, cut up, air-dried. Pasta dates back at least as far as the great days of Rome, for in the museum at Pompeii there is equipment for shaping it.

The pastas used with the sauces we love best are the long strands:
Spaghetti are the familiar tubes sold in varying thicknesses and weights.
Spaghettini are thinner. The thinner the pasta, the higher the identifying number on the box. Thinner pastas are nice with delicate sauces, cook more quickly, and are generally less doughy.
Fettuccine is long, flat pasta with square edges. Two variations on this are the 1/4-inch *taglioni,* and *tagliatelle,* which are a fraction broader than *fettuccine.*
Capellini, or *capelli d'angelo* (angel's air), are very fine, for soups.
Pappardelle are broad and flat, 5/8 inch wide (twice the width of *tagliatelle*), and have edges crimped by the cutting wheel (yes, that's what those wheels are for). Nifty with rich sauces, such as Chicken Liver Sauce, on page 39.
Lasagne are the broadest of the noodles, used almost exclusively for baking.

The pastas used for baking and in salads are lumps of dough hollowed one way or another. The big hollow ones are for stuffing and serving in sauces or in salad platters.
Ziti are the straight, tubes, big and small. Big ones are for stuffing.
Shells, large and small, are pretty in sauces and stuffed for salads.
Macaroni are the familiar half curves, large and small, used in baked cheese dishes and summer salads like the one on page 47. Macaroni also is a general term for all pastas, especially tubular forms.
Rigatoni are big, ridged tubes, usually stuffed and baked.
Tortiglioni (I am mad about the look of these) are shaped like corkscrews and are wonderful in rich sauces and bright summer salads.

These baking pastas are pretty much interchangeable, and all of them take more cooking than the long, thin strands, especially the homemade ones, which cook up in just a few minutes. Commercial pasta sizes are identified by numbers. Strand pastas of similar size and shape also may be used as substitutes.

MAKING YOUR OWN PASTA

When I have cooked pasta briefly—so briefly—just hours after I had made it, I confess I found a whole other world of texture and meltingness. Fresh pasta sold by specialty shops can be really good, too. Worth making from scratch are the pastas for stuffing, like tortellini (little turbans), and ravioli (little pillows, page 22.) And the big noodles, such as lasagna, and the whole wheat pastas, which can be very doughy. A food processor does the mixing and kneading well. If you have a processor, all you need is the patience to rest the dough an hour or two so it can develop real elasticity and to roll it out often enough to make it as thin as it should be (usually as thin as it can be gotten without tearing it). It's a challenge, and that's part of the fun. There are machines for making pasta: For under $50, there are hand-turned machines to roll and cut; for over $100, there are attachments for the good food processors; for over $200, there is one that does everything.

Basic pasta dough is made by the best Italian cooks using 1 1/2 cups wheat flour and 2 large eggs. A tip when working with a pasta machine is to add 1/2 teaspoon salt and 1 tablespoon oil. On pages 22 and 23 you will see two ways to work with this basic recipe: One, mixed by hand, calls for the addition of water; mixed by processor, the same recipe will make a dough without adding water, and that makes a more elastic dough and generally a finer pasta.

Whole wheat pasta is made the same way, but from 3/4 cup whole wheat flour combined with 1/4 cup regular flour, plus whatever more is needed to smooth the dough.

To make *spinach, or green, pasta,* replace 1 of the eggs with 1/2 pound of spinach that has been washed, stemmed, and cooked in 1/4 cup water until just wilted; then drained, chopped, dried over the heat, and incorporate into the basic dough. The next—and vital—step is to rest the dough for 1 to 2 hours under a damp towel, then to roll it out again and again until it is very thin before cutting the desired pasta shapes.

The cut pasta is air-dried—over a broomstick if you wish or a pasta tree. Once it is dry, it stops sticking and can be gathered together, covered, and stored in a cool place for a month or so. Or it can be used at once.

Shells

Macaroni

Tortiglioni

Ziti

Rigatoni

HERBS, VEGETABLES, CHEESES

I AM
oo%
ViRGiN
olive oil

FETTUCCINE WITH SALSA BIANCA

Preparation and cooking time: 20–25 minutes   **Serves 4–6**

Salsa Bianca means "white sauce." In the simple pasta dishes in this section, the sauce is the focal point. Taste as you cook. Add more cream, salt, butter, oil —whatever you like, but with intelligence. Don't add more salt if, for instance, the recipe calls for clam juice later on, because clam juice has lots of salt. Always try a recipe twice—the first time to familiarize yourself with it, the second to suit your own taste.

These pastas are light, ideal for luncheons, for meatless meals, and as the pasta course in a formal Italian meal—the course that is served after the antipasto (hors d'oeuvres in a French meal) and before the entrée. As a pasta course or a side dish for meat or fish, these recipes serve 6. As a main course, they serve 4. When I serve them as a main course, I add salad as an accompaniment, followed by cheese and fruit or by a substantial dessert such as fruit pie or ice cream with melon. I love desserts and serve light main courses to make room for the sweets at the end.

1/2	pound fettuccine	1/4	cup fresh-grated Parmesan cheese
4–5	quarts water	1	tablespoon minced fresh basil or 1/2 teaspoon dried
2	tablespoons salt		
1	tablespoon olive oil	1	tablespoon minced parsley
1/2	cup butter		

In a large covered kettle over high heat, bring the water with the salt to a rapid boil. Add the fettuccine and cook, uncovered, until just tender. Drain.

Meanwhile, in a small saucepan over medium heat, heat the oil. Cut the butter into it a piece at a time and swirl it around, then beat in the cheese, basil, and parsley one at a time. Cook for 1 minute more. Turn into a warmed serving dish. As soon as the fettuccine are drained, toss them with the sauce until well coated and serve at once.

Variation: Pasta al Pesto—Fettuccine in this famous sauce of garlic and tons of basil is one of the most popular pasta dishes. Follow the instructions above, but for the Salsa Bianca substitute the Pesto.

PESTO SAUCE

Preparation time: 15 minutes   **Yield: sauces 6 portions**

You must have a big bunch of fresh basil to make this. Our greengrocer sells his basil with the roots on in spring. I pick the leaves, except for the two bottom ones, and plant the roots in window boxes and tubs near the kitchen—most of them make it, so I keep adding to my basil garden. For salads, I plant several roots of small-leafed basil, which is prettier than the big-leafed basil I use for cooking and stands summer weather without becoming coarse. Ripen Pesto sauce overnight, if you have time. In summer, make the sauce and freeze it for winter when fresh basil is scarce; thaw and remix it in the blender, and add the cheese when you mix it with the hot pasta. Use a tablespoon of it to brighten an undistinguished sauce or salad dressing, just as you use a tablespoon of Pommery or Maille mustard to save a lackluster beef stew.

2	packed cups basil leaves	1	teaspoon salt
3	large garlic cloves	1/4	teaspoon pepper
1/2	cup good olive oil	2	tablespoons butter
1/2	cup pine nuts or chopped walnuts	1/2	cup fresh-grated Parmesan cheese

Put everything but the cheese into a blender or a food processor and process until smooth—5 to 8 minutes. If necessary, use a rubber spatula to push the contents back into the mixer bowl so everything gets mashed finely. Scrape into a glass bowl, cover, and refrigerate if not using at once.

Pour the sauce over just-cooked pasta placed in a warmed serving bowl, sprinkle with cheese, and toss until the cheese is melted.

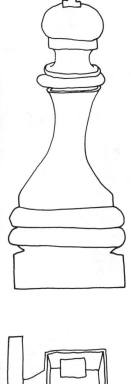

SPINACH FETTUCCINE ALFREDO

Preparation and cooking time: 15–25 minutes   **Serves 4–6**

Spinach fettuccine is a flat noodle that has been flavored (slightly) and colored with the addition of spinach to the dough. It is particularly good when bought fresh-made from a pasta shop, or made in your own kitchen. But the commercially packaged variety, while it is not much different in taste from regular fettuccine, adds a gala touch to a meal. Alfredo sauce is one of the great ones —how can you go wrong with anything so simple? Fresh-grated black pepper is particularly good with this, though I don't advocate grinding pepper over all pasta. Some people do so just because they love big pepper mills, as I do, but though pepper mills are dramatic, pepper doesn't improve everything. If you want to be as fancy as possible with this recipe, make your own sweet butter (see page 9) by beating 1/2 pint of heavy cream until it turns to butter. Can't be fresher than that!

4–5	quarts water	1/2	pint heavy cream
2	tablespoons salt	1	egg yolk
1/2	pound spinach fettuccine	1/2	cup fresh-grated Parmesan
1/2	stick sweet butter		cheese, and more

In a large covered kettle over high heat, bring the water with the salt to a rapid boil. Add the fettuccine, and cook, uncovered, until just tender. Drain.

Meanwhile, melt the butter in a small saucepan over low heat. Turn off the heat. Pour the cream into a small bowl and beat it with the egg yolk until well combined. As soon as the fettuccine are drained, pour the egg-cream mixture over the hot pasta, then the melted butter and half the cheese. Toss gently together, adding more cheese until it is all in. Serve at once, with more grated Parmesan on the side and pass a pepper mill.

MACARONI AND CHEESE

Preparation and cooking time: 45 minutes   Serves 4–5

This elegant version of macaroni and cheese is one to be absolutely mad about! Choose a cheddar you love—mild, medium-mild, or sharp. Great with simple meats that don't add to the kitchen chores by much—hamburgers done some elegant way, with garlic butter, for instance; or, with filet mignon topped with baked mushrooms.

1/2	pound elbow macaroni	2	cups hot milk
4	quarts boiling water	1/2	cup heavy cream
2	tablespoons salt	3/4	pound cheddar cheese,
4	tablespoons butter		grated
3	tablespoons all-purpose		Salt and pepper
	flour		

In a big covered kettle, over high heat, bring the water with the salt to a rapid boil, add the macaroni, and cook, uncovered, until barely tender. Do not overcook! Drain.

Meanwhile, in a large saucepan over low heat, melt the butter, and with a whisk or a fork, stir in the flour to make a smooth paste. Add the hot milk all at once, and stir briskly until the paste and the milk are combined. Raise the heat a little and continue to cook, stirring, until the sauce thickens. Reduce the heat to low and simmer a few minutes more. Turn off the heat, stir in the cream, then two-thirds of the cheese, and stir until the cheese has melted. If necessary, return to low heat to melt the cheese completely. Season with salt and pepper to taste.

Turn the broiler to high.

Stir the drained macaroni into the sauce, then pour into a warmed baking dish, top with the remaining third of the cheese, and put under the broiler for 6 to 10 minutes or just long enough for the sauce to color.

Note: Though this recipe calls for 1/2 pound of elbow macaroni, you may want to cook a whole pound so you'll have a half-pound left over to make macaroni salad for a later meal. (See page 47.)

RIGATONI, FOUR CHEESES, AND HERBS

Preparation and cooking time: 30 minutes   Serves 4–6

This one is the ultimate pasta and cheese recipe. It usually ends with the addition of the four cheeses, but it is better when a little fresh basil or parsley is minced into it. Make and serve the rigatoni with the cheese sauce, and then give each guest sprigs of various fresh herbs, but particularly basil and parsley, to add to the pasta. Two or 3 tip sprigs of each herb is enough. Rigatoni are hollow, ridged, and rather substantial pieces of macaroni, like ziti, designed to hold lots of sauce. This pasta dish is nice with broiled or baked chicken thighs that are seasoned with minced garlic and a little curry powder.

1/8	pound Parmesan cheese	1	pound rigatoni
1/4	pound cold Gruyère	1/2	cup butter
1/4	pound cold Bel Paese		Salt and pepper
1/4	cup cold Gorgonzola	2	tablespoons minced basil
5 to 6	quarts water		or parsley (optional)
2	tablespoons salt		

Grate the Parmesan and Gruyère cheeses into individual bowls by hand or in a food processor. The soft Bel Paese and Gorgonzola (which is like a blue cheese) are easier to grate with a hand grater (you may end up just crumbling the Gorgonzola into bits).

In a large covered kettle over high heat, bring the water and the salt to a rapid boil, and in it cook the rigatoni, uncovered, until barely tender. Drain.

Meanwhile, warm a serving bowl, and in it melt the butter. When the rigatoni are drained, at once toss them in the bowl with the butter, until thoroughly coated. Then, one by one, add the cheeses, tossing well after each addition. Season with salt and pepper to taste, then toss with the minced herbs, if you wish, and serve at once.

SPAGHETTI WITH FRESH TOMATO SAUCE

Preparation and cooking time: 30 minutes   **Serves 4**

This fresh, tangy tomato sauce is wonderful when the pasta is to accompany grilled steaks, broiled fish, hamburgers. Add a green salad and lots of crusty bread to sop up the gravy! Since the flavor depends on the tomatoes, use only garden-ripened, dense plum varieties—really flavorful tomatoes. If that kind of tomato isn't available, then make this with a 16-ounce can of plum tomatoes or tomatoes in tomato puree.

4–5 quarts of water	3 large garlic cloves, sliced
2 tablespoons salt	1/4 cup olive oil
1/2 pound spaghetti	1/4 teaspoon salt
1 small bunch fresh basil	1/8 teaspoon pepper
1 pound plum tomatoes, or enough to make 2 cups, chopped	Salt and pepper

In a big covered kettle over high heat, bring the water with the salt to a rapid boil, and in it cook the spaghetti, uncovered, until just tender. Drain.

Meanwhile, rinse and air-dry the basil, pick off all the leaves, and process them in a food processor or a blender, with the tomatoes and the garlic, just enough to chop the basil. Heat a big, heavy skillet over medium-high heat and in it warm the oil. Sauté the tomato mixture, seasoned with the salt and pepper, until it comes to a rapid boil, then reduce the heat and simmer gently until the spaghetti is ready—the sauce should cook a total of about 15 minutes. Taste, and add more salt and pepper if needed. Turn the sauce into a warmed serving dish, and in it toss the drained spaghetti.

Variation: Tomato Sauce with Cream—To the completed Tomato Sauce add 1/2 cup heavy cream and toss the spaghetti in it at once.

FETTUCCINE WITH ASPARAGUS IN BASIL CREAM

Preparation and cooking time: 45 minutes　　　　　Serves 4–6

This makes a great meatless supper or a wonderful side dish for grilled meats. It's substantial, so serve with it a very light salad and dessert.

16	medium asparagus	1/2	bunch parsley leaves,
	Water		minced fine (1/2 cup)
2	tablespoons salt	3/4	cup heavy cream
8	ounces fettuccine	1	cup fresh-grated Parmesan
2	tablespoons olive oil		cheese
2	large garlic cloves	1	teaspoon salt
1/2	packed cup basil, minced	1/4	teaspoon black pepper
	fine		

Rinse the asparagus and bend the bottoms till they snap off. Discard bottoms. Cut the tops into 1-inch pieces. Prepare all the other ingredients.

Place two big kettles over high heat, the first with 6 quarts of water, the second with 3 quarts. Add 1 tablespoon salt to each kettle, and cover. When the first boils, put into it the fettuccine and cook, uncovered, until barely tender. Drain. When the second boils, add all the asparagus pieces to it, reduce the heat to medium, and cook, uncovered, for about 6 minutes. Drain when asparagus is just tender but still dark green.

While these two ingredients are cooking, heat the olive oil in a large skillet over medium heat, crush the garlic into it and sauté for 1 minute. Add the basil and parsley, and sauté for 2 minutes, stirring. Reduce the heat, toss the asparagus pieces in the oil-and-herb mixture, then turn the just-drained fettuccine into the mixture and toss again. Transfer to a heated serving dish and keep warm.

In a small saucepan over medium heat, bring the cream to simmering and stir the grated Parmesan into it. When the cheese has dissolved and the cream thickened, stir in the salt and pepper and pour the sauce over the asparagus and pasta. Toss well, and serve at once.

TORTIGLIONI IN RATATOUILLE SAUCE

Preparation and cooking time: 45 minutes   **Serves 4–6**

Tortiglioni, like rotelle and fusille, are pasta twists, ideal for holding lots of sauce. All sorts of vegetables can go into it—beans, summer squash, fall broccoli. If you have lots of garden-ripened tomatoes, double the quantity called for here and omit the tomato paste. Tomato paste is what we add when we are dealing with city tomatoes.

3	tablespoons olive oil	6	tip sprigs each of fresh thyme, rosemary, oregano, basil, parsley
2	large garlic cloves		
1/4	large Bermuda onion		
3	tablespoons tomato paste (see above)	12–15	pitted ripe olives, sliced into 1/4-inch rounds
4	large ripe tomatoes	4–5	quarts water
1	small eggplant, peeled	2	tablespoons salt
1	small zucchini, skinned	2	cups tortiglioni or shell macaroni
1/2	green pepper, seeded		
1	teaspoon salt	1/2	cup fresh-grated Parmesan cheese
1/8	teaspoon pepper		
1/2	teaspoon sugar		

Set a big, heavy saucepan over medium heat. Heat the oil in it, and mince the garlic into it. Slice the onion in thick strips over the garlic. When the onions have softened, stir in the tomato paste. Cut the vegetables into 2-inch chunks and add. Stir in the salt, pepper, sugar; mince the herbs into the pot, and add the olives. Reduce the heat and simmer gently until the tomatoes are cooked and the sauce is thick—10 or 15 minutes. Turn off the heat.

Meanwhile, in a large covered kettle over high heat, bring the water with the salt to a rapid boil, and in it cook the tortiglioni or shell macaroni, uncovered, until just tender. Drain, and turn into the vegetable mélange. Toss three or four times with the vegetables, then sprinkle the cheese over the mixture and toss several times more.

TORTELLINI AL PESTO WITH MOZZARELLA

Preparation time: 15 minutes   **Serves 4**

Pesto Sauce, page 13, is made of basil, oil, pine nuts, and cheese, creating a really gutsy flavor as intense as Snail Butter (see *Mad About Mushrooms*). The little tortellini—stuffed, ring-shape dumplings—are available in supermarkets and in specialty shops. This is a delightful combination. The mozzarella makes it a really substantial dish, ideal for a meatless supper. It's nice with crusty bread and a very simple salad of tossed greens.

1/2	recipe Pesto Sauce, (p. 13)	8	ounces mozzarella cheese
4	quarts water		salt and pepper
2	tablespoons salt	24	slices thin garlic sausage
8	ounces cheese tortellini		Tomatoes (optional)

Prepare the Pesto Sauce, up to the addition of the cheese.

In a big covered kettle over high heat, bring the water with the salt to a rapid boil and in it cook the tortellini, uncovered, until just tender. Meanwhile, dice the mozzarella and set a serving dish to warm.

Drain the tortellini and pour two-thirds of the Pesto Sauce over them, and half of the Parmesan cheese called for in the Pesto recipe. Toss the tortellini, the sauce, and the cheese together until the tortellini are well coated and the cheese is melted. Taste, and add more Pesto and cheese if you wish. Cover the tortellini with the diced mozzarella and toss again just before serving. Garnish with sausage slices folded in four. If you have garden-fresh ripe tomatoes, slice them into rounds 1/4 inch thick and stand around the plate.

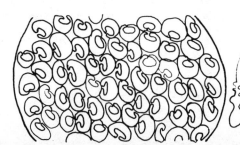

FETTUCCINE WITH MUSHROOM SAUCE

Preparation and cooking time: 30 minutes   **Serves 4**

The ultimate mushroom flavor—nifty with grilled steaks and a salad. (For scrumptious mushroom recipes, see *Mad About Mushrooms*.)

12 ounces mushrooms	1/2 cup bottled clam juice
4 tablespoons butter	1/2 cup heavy cream
1 large garlic clove, minced	4–5 quarts water
1 green onion, trimmed and minced	2 tablespoons salt
1/2 teaspoon grated lemon rind	1/2 pound fettuccine
1/2 teaspoon salt	4 sprigs fresh thyme, basil, or parsley, minced
1 tablespoon all-purpose flour	

Clean the mushrooms with a damp paper towel and remove the tough ends of the stems. For a third of the mushrooms, bend the stems until they break; reserve the stems. In a large skillet over medium-high heat, melt the butter and add the garlic and onion. Cut the mushroom caps into 1/4-inch-thick slices and add to the skillet; sauté for 2 minutes. Turn off the heat, and, using a slotted spoon, remove the mushrooms to a small bowl. Reserve.

Chop the reserved stems and remaining mushrooms in a food processor, a blender, or by hand. Reheat the skillet to medium high and in it sauté the chopped mushrooms for 4 minutes, stirring. Turn the heat to low. Stir in the lemon rind, salt, and flour to make a smooth mixture, then add the clam juice and cream all at once and stir until a smooth sauce forms. Simmer for 4 or 5 minutes; place in a serving bowl for pasta.

In a big covered kettle over high heat, bring the water with the salt to a rapid boil and in it cook the fettuccine, uncovered, until just tender. Drain. Toss the fettuccine in the mushroom sauce, garnish with the reserved mushroom slices, and add the minced thyme, basil, or parsley. Serve and pass the pepper mill.

SPINACH AND CHEESE RAVIOLI WITH SALSA BIANCA

Preparation time: 1–1 1/2 hours
Completion time: 20 minutes   **Serves 6**

Ravioli are stuffed pasta, dumpling-like casings of thin dough—round, as here, or square filled with ricotta or other cheeses. Homemade, and worth the fuss! If you have a pasta machine and ravioli forms, use them. This recipe tells how to make your own pasta, and ravioli, without.

3	cups all-purpose flour		4–5	quarts water
1/2	teaspoon salt		2	tablespoons salt
2	eggs, slightly beaten		1	tablespoon oil
3/4-1	cup water, if needed		1	recipe Salsa Bianca
	Spinach Filling (p. 23)			(see p. 12)

Combine the flour and salt in a processor or mixing bowl. If you are using a processor, add the eggs, and process.

If the processor kneads this into dough without water, omit water. If not, add water by the teaspoonful to the processor bowl as it beats the dough, just enough water to make a dough ball, then process 10 minutes.

If working with a mixing bowl and by hand, make a well in the center of the flour-salt mixture and pour in the eggs mixed with 1/4 cup of water at room temperature. Stir with your fingers until the liquids have picked up enough flour to form a dough. Add 1/4 cup of water and continue stirring, working to absorb into the dough ball the remaining flour. If needed, add another 1/4 cup of water or more, until all the flour is in the dough. Flour the counter or a cutting board, and work the dough, kneading it under the heels of your hands, and rolling it away from you, 5 to 10 minutes, or until it is quite elastic and beginning to feel silky, like nice skin. Cover with a damp cloth and rest an hour or 2.

Prepare the Spinach Filling as directed, and chill.

Flour the board again, and a rolling pin. Roll out the dough again and again, until it is quite thin. This will take a little doing, because it will be very elastic. With a cookie cutter, or a glass rubbed in flour, cut 3-inch circles in the dough.

Spoon a dab of Spinach Filling into the center of each circle. Fold over into half-circles and, with a wet fork, crimp around the edges on all sides to seal the edges together. Keep the ravioli on a floured tray. Do not heap them or they will stick together. The ravioli can now rest several hours or overnight, in a cool place.

In a big covered kettle over high heat, bring the water with the salt and the oil to a rapid boil. Dump the ravioli into the kettle all at once, reduce the heat and stir with a big spoon to keep it from sticking as the ravioli simmers. Cook for 10 to 12 minutes, and eat one to see if it is tender. Cook another minute if necessary. Drain.

While the ravioli cooks, prepare the Salsa Bianca, and turn it into a warm serving bowl. Toss the drained ravioli in the sauce. Serve.

SPINACH FILLING

Preparation time: 15 minutes

4	cups washed spinach	1	large garlic clove, crushed
1	egg, slightly beaten	1	teaspoon minced parsley
1/4	cup fresh-grated Parmesan cheese	1/2	teaspoon minced fresh basil
1/4	cup Mozzarella cheese	1/8	teaspoon oregano
1/4	cup ricotta cheese		Salt and pepper

Turn the spinach into a large, heavy saucepan, set over high heat, cover tightly, and cook until the spinach has completely wilted—but don't cook till it loses its color—3 to 5 minutes. Drain in a colander, press out the water, and return to the kettle. Shake over heat to dry the spinach. Chop a little to cut thick stems, then beat the remaining ingredients into the spinach. Season with and add salt and pepper to taste. Beat another moment, then chill until ready to use.

SEA SAUCES

SPAGHETTINI WITH WHITE CLAM SAUCE

Preparation and cooking time: 30–40 minutes　　　　**Serves 4–6**

Seafood pastas are great only when the fish or shellfish is fresh. You can make this with canned clams and clam juice, but it will—merely be good. Use fresh basil, too. As a first course, this recipe will serve six; as a main course, it makes a satisfying dinner for four if you add a hearty salad, hot crusty French bread and butter (you need bread to sop up this delicious sauce), and a substantial dessert.

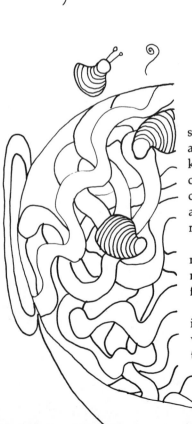

12	cherrystone (3-inch) clams
12	littleneck (1 1/2-inch) clams (optional)
1/2	cup butter
3	large garlic cloves
1/2	teaspoon dried or 1 teaspoon fresh oregano

1	tablespoon minced basil
1	tablespoon minced parsley
4–5	quarts water
2	tablespoons salt
1	pound spaghettini

Heat the oven to 400°. Scrub the clams to remove all sand. Set the cherrystones in a baking dish in the hot oven for 5 minutes; add the littlenecks, if you are using them, and heat for 5 minutes more or until all are open. Insert a sharp knife into each of the large clams, split them open, and remove the clam. Discard the shells. Open but do not split the small clams and reserve them. Save the clam juices, and pour into a measuring cup; you should have about 1 cup. If not, add a little water or pour off a little. By hand, coarsely chop the big clams and reserve them.

In a small saucepan over medium heat, melt the butter and into it finely mince the garlic. Stir in the reserved clam juice and the oregano and cook for 5 minutes over high heat. Add the chopped clams, basil, and parsley and simmer for 5 minutes more. Turn off the heat.

In a big covered kettle over high heat, bring the water with the salt to a rapid boil and in it cook the spaghettini, uncovered, until barely tender. Drain. Divide the spaghettini among 4 or 6 soup bowls and pour the clam sauce over them. Garnish with small clams. Serve.

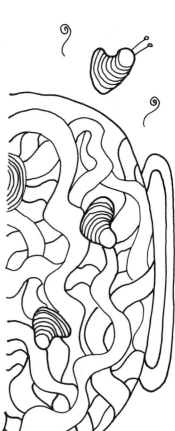

Variation: Whole Wheat Spaghetti in Red Clam Sauce—Made in a manner similar to the recipe for Spaghettini with White Clam Sauce, but the sauce is based on olive oil and tomatoes rather than butter, herbs, and clams, following the recipe below. You will need 2/3 pound of whole wheat pasta, which is very substantial. Cook it until *tender*.

RED CLAM SAUCE

Preparation and cooking time: 30–40 minutes   **Serves 4–6**

This is another delicious sauce made by good Italian restaurants. I especially like it with lasagna, (see page 26), but it is great with spaghettini, too. In this recipe, the tomato flavor dominates, so having fresh clams is not quite as crucial as when you are making White Clam Sauce.

12 cherrystone clams, minced, or 3 eight-ounce cans minced clams	1/2 teaspoon dried or 1 teaspoon fresh oregano, minced
2 large garlic cloves, minced	1 tablespoon minced basil
1/4 cup olive oil 29-ounce can tomatoes in tomato puree	1 tablespoon minced parsley

If using fresh clams, heat the oven to 400°. Scrub the clams to remove all sand. Set them in a baking dish in the hot oven for 8 to 10 minutes or until all the clams are open. Insert a sharp knife into each clam, split it open, remove the clam. Discard the shells, taking care to preserve the clam juices. By hand, coarsely chop the clams and reserve them.

If you are using canned minced clams, drain and reserve the juice and reserve the clams.

In a large saucepan over medium heat, sauté the garlic in the oil for 1 or 2 minutes. Add the tomatoes and the puree. Slightly crush the tomatoes. Stir in the herbs and the reserved clam juice. Simmer for 20 to 30 minutes, or until the sauce thickens. Stir in the clams and serve.

LASAGNA WITH RED CLAM SAUCE

Preparation time: about 1 hour
Baking time: 40 minutes   Serves 8–10

Lasagne are broad egg noodles for baked dishes. This delicious, meatless recipe is featured on our cover and may be made a day ahead and baked before serving. Thick doughs, such as lasagna and the whole wheat noodles, are really better if fresh or homemade. (They'll cook half as long as here.)

1	recipe Red Clam Sauce (p. 25)	1/2	cup fresh-grated Parmesan cheese, and more
1	pound lasagna	2	tablespoons minced basil or parsley
5–6	quarts water	1	teaspoon salt
2	tablespoons salt	1/4	teaspoon pepper
1	tablespoon oil	1	pound mozzarella cheese
2	cups ricotta cheese		
2	eggs, beaten		

Prepare the Red Clam Sauce.

In a big covered kettle over high heat, bring the water with the salt and oil to a rapid boil and in it cook the lasagna, uncovered, until just barely tender. As it cooks, separate the strands with a wooden spoon. Drain and cover with cold water.

Heat the oven to 400°. In a 13- or 15-inch-long rectangular baking dish, assemble the lasagna: Ladle a spoonful of Red Clam Sauce into the bottom of the dish and spread it around. One at a time, lift three or four lasagna strips from the water, drain, then place in the dish side by side so they cover the bottom. In a medium bowl, beat the ricotta with the eggs and the Parmesan cheese, basil or parsley, and salt. Smooth half the mixture over the lasagna. Cover with a layer of lasagna strips, ladle half of the remaining sauce over the lasagna, grate two-thirds of the mozzarella over the sauce. Cover with a layer of lasagna strips. Spread the last of the sauce over the top layer of lasagna, and sprinkle the remaining mozzarella over the sauce.

Bake for 20 minutes, and allow to settle outside the oven 15 minutes before serving. Offer Parmesan with the lasagna, and a pepper mill.

SPAGHETTINI WITH MARINARA SAUCE

Preparation and cooking time: 45 minutes   Serves 4–6

The first time I cooked this, I thought to myself, "Aha! *This* is the aroma that greets you in a good little Italian restaurant!" It's another of those fast, great, simple Italian sauces that make the cook feel like a genius. If you can't find tomatoes in thick puree, use whole tomatoes and add 2 tablespoons tomato paste to the contents of the can. This sauce may be made a few hours ahead and reheated when the pasta is ready. *Marinara* means "from the sea," and you can build others on the basic recipe—add half a dozen clams, for instance. Marinara is a great sauce to serve over fish.

4	tablespoons olive oil	1/2	teaspoon salt
2	medium onions, chopped	1	teaspoon fresh oregano or
2	large garlic cloves, minced		1/2 teaspoon dried
4	flat anchovy fillets	1/2	teaspoon sugar
	29-ounce can whole toma-	4–5	quarts water
	toes in puree	2	tablespoons salt
1/2	cup dry white wine or	1/2–2/3	pound spaghettini
	bottled clam juice		

In a large enameled saucepan or casserole over medium-high heat, heat the oil and in it sauté the onions and the garlic. Cook and stir about 5 or 6 minutes, until the onions are translucent. Add the anchovies, stirring them around until they begin to break up. Add the canned tomatoes and puree, the wine or clam juice, salt, oregano, and sugar, and bring to a boil. Break up the tomatoes and continue cooking over medium-low heat, uncovered, stirring often, for 25 to 30 minutes. The sauce will thicken. If it is becoming dry, reduce the heat to low and continue to cook, covered.

In a big covered kettle over high heat, bring the water and the salt to a rapid boil and in it cook the spaghettini, uncovered, until just tender. Drain. Turn the completed sauce into a warmed serving dish. In it toss the just-drained pasta. Serve.

SPAGHETTINI WITH MUSSELS IN WINE SAUCE

Preparation time: 30–40 minutes   **Serves 4**

If you like mussels, you will love this! One caution: the mussels must be well scrubbed. You *must* snap each one between thumb and forefinger—that will split the shells if they are filled with sand instead of fish. And you *must* scrape off every last barnacle and bit of seaweed with a sharp knife or they will fall into the cooked sauce. Some markets sell really well-cleaned mussels, and others do not. So look closely at what you are buying.

2–3	pounds medium mussels	1/2	small bay leaf
1/4	cup minced shallots or green onions	1	cup dry white wine
		1	tablespoon minced parsley
1/2	cup butter	4–5	quarts water
2	tablespoons minced parsley	2	tablespoons salt
1/2	teaspoon dried thyme	1/2	pound spaghettini

In cold running water, scrub and scrape the mussels as described and drain them. Leave them in a colander.

In a big kettle sauté the shallots in half the butter over medium heat until translucent—about 5 minutes. Add the mussels, 2 tablespoons of parsley, thyme, bay leaf, crumbled, and wine. Cover the kettle, raise the heat, and bring to a simmer, then reduce the heat and simmer for 4 to 8 minutes, shaking the pan often, until all the mussels are open. Pour the mussels into a big, warm serving dish, keeping the sauce in the kettle.

Meanwhile, in another big covered kettle, bring the water and the salt to a rapid boil over high heat, and then cook the pasta, uncovered, until just tender.

Drain the pasta and toss with the mussels. Melt the remaining butter in the mussel-cooking kettle, and when it is frothing, stir in the 1 tablespoon of minced parsley. Stir and cook for 30 seconds, and pour over the spaghettini. Toss well and serve at once.

FETTUCCINE WITH MUSSELS CLÉMENCE

Preparation and cooking time: 45 minutes   **Serves 4–6**

Clémence was my French grandmother. I inherited my faith in butter, cream, and garlic from her. Mussels are still offered in shining indigo heaps in the big farmers' markets in Les Sables d'Olonne, the fishing village the Hériteaux come from. Matching piles of shiny blue-black mussels are now becoming available in New York through small fish stores such as the Jumbo Fish Market, and others run by new Americans.

2–3 pounds medium-size mussels	1 tablespoon minced garlic
4–5 quarts water	1/3 cup minced parsley
2 tablespoons salt	2 tablespoons butter
1/2–2/3 pound fettuccine	1/2 cup heavy cream
6 tablespoons olive oil	1 tablespoon minced basil

Scrub and scrape the mussels in cold running water, as described on page 28. Leave them draining in a colander. Bring the water and the salt to a rapid boil in a big covered kettle over high heat and cook the fettuccine in it, uncovered, until barely tender. Drain. Spread 2 tablespoons oil in the bottom of a warm serving dish and toss the fettuccine in it.

Meanwhile, in another big covered kettle that has a lid that fits fairly tightly, heat the remaining oil over medium heat, and sauté the garlic and the parsley in it for 1 or 2 minutes—just enough to color the garlic; then add the mussels, cover tightly, and shake and cook over high heat until all the mussels are open. Remove the top shell from half the mussels. With a slotted spoon, scoop all the mussels over the fettuccine.

Pour the mussel cooking broth into a cup, and measure the amount. Return it to the kettle and boil down to half, then stir in the butter and cream and bring to boiling. Simmer for a minute or so until the sauce thickens a bit, stir in the basil, and simmer for 30 seconds more. Pour over the fettucine and toss together. Serve at once.

SPAGHETTINI WITH SCAMPI SAUCE

Preparation and cooking time: 35–45 minutes   Serves 4–6

This is heaven made with the tiny shrimp we sometimes find on Cape Cod, on trucks fishermen bring down overnight from Maine. But regular-size shrimp (easier to shell by far!) make very good sauce, too! With a tossed salad, bread, cheese, and fruit, this is a delicious light meal.

1	pound regular-size shrimp	1	teaspoon minced thyme
2	tablespoons lemon juice	4–5	quarts water
1/3	cup olive oil	2	tablespoons salt
3	large garlic cloves, minced	1/2–2/3	pound spaghettini
	29-ounce can whole tomatoes in puree	2	tablespoons minced parsley
1/4	teaspoon salt	1	tablespoon minced basil
1/8	teaspon pepper	1	basil sprig
1	teaspoon minced oregano		

Shell, devein, and rinse the shrimp; place them in a bowl and sprinkle with the lemon juice.

In a large heavy saucepan over medium heat, heat the oil and sauté the garlic for 1 minute. Stir in the tomatoes and puree, and slightly mash the tomatoes. Season with salt and pepper, oregano, and thyme, and simmer, stirring now and then, for 15 minutes.

Meanwhile, in a big covered kettle over high heat, bring the water with the salt to a rapid boil and in it cook the spaghettini, uncovered, until just tender. Drain.

Just before you drain the pasta, stir the shrimp, parsley, and minced basil into the tomato mixture and cook for 3 minutes. Put in a warm serving dish. Add the drained pasta to the dish and toss together several times. Bring a few good-looking shrimp to the top of the pasta heap, garnish with a sprig of basil, and serve at once.

TORTIGLIONI WITH RED SNAPPER SAUCE

Preparation and cooking time: 25–35 minutes　　　　　　**Serves 4**

This is excellent made with any similar fish—striped bass, for instance—but not with strongly flavored fish such as mackerel. Serve a tomato-and-green-pepper salad with it, bread, cheese, and dessert.

4–5 quarts water	1 large red snapper fillet
2 tablespoons salt	(1/3–1/2 pound)
1/2 pound tortiglioni	1 teaspoon grated lemon
2 tablespoons butter	rind
1 tablespoon olive oil	1/2 teaspoon salt
4 tablespoons butter	1/4 teaspoon pepper
Bunch green onions,	1/2 cup heavy cream
trimmed and minced	2 tablespoons parsley
1 large garlic clove, minced	4 lemon wedges

In a big covered kettle over high heat, bring the water with the salt to a rapid boil and cook the tortiglioni in it, uncovered, until barely tender. While it cooks, warm the butter in a serving dish for pasta. Drain the *pasta* and place in the warmed serving dish.

Meanwhile, in a large heavy skillet over medium heat, warm the oil and melt the 4 tablespoons of butter in it. Add the onions and the garlic, and while it is still frothing, slide the fish fillet into the skillet. Shake the pan often as it cooks for 3 minutes. Season the fish with the lemon rind, salt, and pepper. Turn it over carefully and cook for another 2 minutes. Turn off the heat and pour the cream into the pan at once, scraping up the pan juices with a spatula as it simmers down. The fish will break up into big flakes as you stir. Sprinkle parsley over the fish, stir once more, and scrape over the pasta. Toss together before serving. Garnish with lemon wedges.

TORTIGLIONI WITH SCALLOPS AND CREAM

Preparation and cooking time: 30–40 minutes   **Serves 4**

The little bay scallops are my preference for this recipe, and I use tortiglioni, the twisty pasta, because it takes up a lot of sauce with each bite—and the sauce is so subtle and so good! Nice with a salad of Boston or Bibb lettuce or green oak-leaf lettuce from the garden, and tart fresh fruit for dessert.

1	small onion, minced	1/8	teaspoon pepper
1	stalk celery, minced	1/2	cup dry white wine
1	small carrot, minced	1/2	pound bay scallops
4	sprigs parsley, minced	1	cup heavy cream
1	large leek, cut in thin strips	1	tablespoon minced parsley
4	tablespoons butter	4–5	quarts water
1	small bay leaf	2	tablespoons salt
1	teaspoon minced fresh thyme or 1/2 teaspoon dried	2	cups tortiglioni
		1	tablespoon minced parsley
1/2	teaspoon salt	1	cup fresh-grated Parmesan cheese

In a large saucepan over medium heat, sauté the onion, celery, carrot, parsley, and leek in half the butter with the bay leaf, thyme, salt, and pepper for 8 minutes, stirring. Stir in the wine and simmer for 8 minutes more. Stir in the scallops and the remaining 2 tablespoons of butter, and cook for 1 minute. Add the cream and parsley, scraping up the pan juices, and cook 1 minute more. Pour onto a warmed serving dish.

Meanwhile, in a big covered kettle over high heat, bring the water with the salt to a rapid boil, and in it cook the tortiglioni, uncovered, until tender. Drain, add to the scallop sauce, and toss well, bringing a few choice scallops to the top. Sprinkle with parsley and serve at once. Pass Parmesan cheese and a pepper mill.

FETTUCCINE WITH LOBSTER SAUCE

Preparation and cooking time: 35–45 minutes   **Serves 4**

If you like bouillabaisse, you'll love this exotic combination of saffron, anise, orange rind, and lobster. It's nice with champagne or a nonalcoholic, bubbly, light celebratory something.

1	rock lobster tail (about 1 pound) or 16 ounces canned	1/4	teaspoon anise seeds
		1/4	teaspoon saffron threads
		1/2	teaspoon salt
1/4	cup olive oil	1/4	teaspoon pepper
4	green onions, trimmed and minced	1	teaspoon grated orange rind
1 1/2	large clove garlic	4–5	quarts water
3/4	cup canned crushed, tomatoes	2	tablespoons salt
		1/2	pound fettuccine
4	ounces bottled clam juice	4	sprigs parsley

Thaw the lobster tail enough to shell it. Set the tail on its back and cut down the center. Break the shell in half, pull out the two strips of lobster meat, and cut into 1/4-inch strips. If using canned lobster, drain, reserving the juices; remove any cartilage and break up the meat.

In a large, heavy saucepan over medium heat, heat the oil, and sauté the onions in it until they begin to brown—6 to 7 minutes. Slice the garlic into the onions, then stir in the tomatoes, clam juice, anise, saffron, salt, pepper, and orange rind. Simmer, uncovered, for 5 minutes. Add the lobster pieces and juices and simmer for another 5 minutes.

Meanwhile, in a big covered kettle over high heat, bring the water with the salt to a rapid boil and cook the fettuccine in it, uncovered, until just tender. Drain.

Pour the lobster sauce into a warm serving dish and toss the fettuccine in the sauce. Garnish with sprigs of parsley.

MEAT AND CHICKEN SAUCES

BOLOGNESE SAUCE

Preparation time: 30 minutes
Cooking time: 2–5 hours

Yield: Sauce for 4–6 portions

In this section, you will find the meaty pastas that make main courses. Bolognese is the great classic meat sauce from Bologna—best when it cooks for hours in a crock pot. However, it is really good even when you cook it just a couple of hours on top of the stove at a slow simmer. This recipe will sauce 1/2 to 2/3 pound of spaghettini.

3	tablespoons butter		1/4	teaspoon black pepper
3	tablespoons olive oil		1	pound lean ground round
1	large clove garlic		1	cup dry white wine
1	medium onion		1/2	cup milk
1	large carrot			28-ounce can peeled plum
2	sprigs fresh basil or 1/2			tomatoes
	teaspoon dried		1/2	cup heavy cream
1	teaspoon salt			Salt and pepper

In a big, heavy skillet over medium heat, melt the butter in the oil, and mince into the skillet the garlic, onion, and carrot. Stir in the basil, salt, and pepper and cook for 2 or 3 minutes. Mash in the ground meat and stir and cook until it is browned, then pour in the wine and stir until all the moisture has evaporated. Stir in the milk and cook until that moisture no longer shows. Then mash in the tomatoes, cover, reduce the heat to very low, and simmer for 2 hours. Or transfer to an electric crock pot and simmer on low for 4 to 5 hours.

Just before serving, stir in the cream and cook for 2 minutes more. Season with salt and pepper to taste.

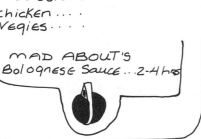

Variation: Lasagne Verdi and Bolognese Sauce—One of the great combinations is spinach or green lasagna baked with Bolognese Sauce. Follow the recipe for Lasagna with Bolognese Sauce, page 36, but substitute green lasagna for regular lasagna.

MEAT SAUCE WITH TOMATOES

Preparation and cooking time: 50–60 minutes   **Yield: Sauce for
                                                        4–6 portions**

This is the first sauce I learned to make for pasta. It is spicy and hearty, and kids love it over spaghetti and in lasagna dishes. This will sauce 1/2 to 2/3 pound of pasta.

3 tablespoons olive oil	2 large green peppers, seeded and chopped
1 large onion, chopped	
2 large garlic cloves, sliced	2 large stalks celery, diced
1 1/2 pounds ground round	1/2 pound small mushrooms, cut in half
16-ounce can whole plum tomatoes	
6-ounce can tomato paste diluted in 2/3 cup water	2 teaspoons salt
	1/4 teaspoon pepper
1 teaspoon sugar	1/4 cup fresh-grated Parmesan cheese and more
1 teaspoon dried basil	
1 teaspoon dried oregano	2 tablespoons sweet butter

Set a large heavy skillet over medium-high heat. Heat the oil and sauté the onion and the garlic in it until the onion is really browned but not burned.

Mash the meat into the hot oil and sauté it, breaking it up and turning it often until it is in little lumps and browned. Stir the tomatoes into the skillet, scraping up the pan juices, then the tomato paste diluted in the water. Reduce the heat to low and stir in the sugar, herbs, pepper, celery, and mushrooms. Season with salt and pepper, cover, and simmer for 30 to 45 minutes. Stir in the Parmesan and butter, and turn into a warmed serving dish. Toss with the cooked pasta. Offer more Parmesan and the pepper mill.

LASAGNA WITH BOLOGNESE SAUCE

Preparation and baking time: 1 hour   **Serves 8–10**

This is northern Italian, the sophisticated lasagna.

1	recipe Bolognese Sauce (p. 34)	4–5	quarts water
6	tablespoons unsalted butter	2	tablespoons salt
4	tablespoons all-purpose flour	1	tablespoon oil
2	cups hot milk and more	1	pound lasagna
1/2	teaspoon salt	1	cup fresh-grated Parmesan cheese
	Pinch nutmeg	3	tablespoons butter
		4	sprigs basil, or parsley

Prepare the Bolognese Sauce. When it is half cooked, melt the butter in a large enameled saucepan over low heat, and stir in the flour with a whisk to make a smooth paste. Pour in 2 cups of hot milk all at once, and beat rapidly to smooth out the sauce. Stir in salt and a pinch of nutmeg. Cook until the sauce thickens, then turn off the heat. It will continue to thicken in its own heat.

In a big covered kettle over high heat, bring the water with the salt and the oil to a rapid boil. In it cook the lasagna, uncovered, until barely tender. As it cooks, separate the strands with a spoon. Drain and fill the kettle with enough cold water to cover the lasagna.

Preheat the oven to 450°. In a 13- or 15-inch-long rectangular baking pan, assemble the lasagna: Ladle a spoonful of the completed Bolognese Sauce into the bottom of the dish and spread it around. One at a time, lift three or four lasagna strips from the water, drain, then place in the pan side by side so they cover the bottom. Spread a thin layer of Bolognese over the pasta. Dip a ladle or a big spoon into the cream sauce, and if it is too thick to pour easily, thin it with enough milk to achieve a thick but pourable sauce. Spread a thin layer of this sauce over the layer of noodles, and cover with a little Parmesan. Cover with a layer of lasagna strips, and repeat the sauces and the cheese. Build the layers to within 1/2 inch of the top of the dish. Cover the top layer with the last of the cream sauce, sprinkle with 1/4 cup of the Parmesan, dot with butter.

Bake the lasagna for 10 to 15 minutes—just long enough for the top to color and crust a little. Allow to settle outside the oven for 10 to 15 minutes before serving. Garnish with a few sprigs of green herb, and pass more Parmesan and the pepper mill when serving.

LASAGNA WITH MEAT SAUCE

Preparation time: 1 hour
Baking time: 40 minutes   **Serves 8–10**

1 recipe Meat Sauce with Tomatoes (p. 35)	2 pounds large-curd cottage cheese
6 Italian sausages, hot	1/2 pound mozzarella cheese
1 pound lasagna, cooked (see p. 36)	1/2 cup fresh-grated Parmesan cheese
	2 tablespoons minced basil

Prepare the Meat Sauce, browning the sausages called for here with the meat. Cook the lasagna as described for Lasagna with Bolognese Sauce.

Preheat the oven to 450°. In a 15-inch rectangular baking pan, assemble the lasagna: Ladle a spoonful of the Meat Sauce, reserving the sausages, over the bottom of the pan, and spread it around. One at a time, lift three or four strips of lasagna from the water, drain, then place in the pan side by side so they cover the bottom. Spread half the cottage cheese over the lasagna. Over this, spoon a third of the remaining sauce, and grate over it half the mozzarella. Slice the sausages thin and cover the mozzarella with half the sausage slices. Cover with another layer of lasagna. Repeat. Top with lasagna, cover with the remainder of the sauce, and 1/2 cup grated Parmesan.

Bake the lasagna for 20 minutes, or until the top has browned. Allow to settle outside the oven 10 to 15 minutes before serving. Garnish with fresh basil.

SPAGHETTINI CARBONARA

Preparation and cooking time: 20–30 minutes   **Serves 4–6**

Prosciutto is a ham (cured pork) specialty from Italy, staggeringly expensive, refined in taste, and essential now and then to wrap around ripe cantaloupe as an hors d'oeuvre. Spaghettini Carbonara may also be made with bacon, and I find bacon lovers prefer it that way.

4–5	quarts water	3	large eggs, slightly beaten
2	tablespoons salt	3	tablespoons heavy cream
1	pound spaghettini	1/2	cup fresh-grated Romano cheese
2	tablespoons olive oil	1/2	cup fresh-grated Parmesan cheese
1	tablespoon butter		Pinch black pepper
4	large cloves garlic	3	tablespoons minced parsley
1/2	pound prosciutto or good bacon, minced		
1/4	cup dry white wine		

In a big covered kettle over high heat, bring the water with the salt to a rapid boil and in it cook the spaghettini, uncovered, until just tender. Drain.

Meanwhile, working quickly enough to finish the sauce *before* the pasta is cooked (spaghettini cook quickly), heat the oil and butter in a large skillet over high heat, mince the garlic into it and stir for 2 minutes, then stir in the prosciutto or bacon pieces and stir and fry until they are crisp. Reduce the heat to medium, stir in the wine, and simmer until the moisture evaporates. Turn off the heat.

Beat the eggs with the cream in a bowl and turn into a slightly warmed serving dish just before the spaghettini are drained. Turn the hot, just-drained spaghettini into the egg mixture and quickly toss with the eggs, lifting the pasta high as you toss. Sprinkle with Romano and toss twice. Sprinkle with Parmesan and toss twice more. Grate black pepper over the pasta, scrape the sauce in the skillet over it, and garnish with minced parsley. Just before serving, toss again.

PAPPARDELLE WITH CHICKEN LIVER SAUCE

Preparation and cooking time: 30 minutes   **Serves 4**

Pappardella is a long noodle with a crimped edge, about a half-inch wide. Tagliatelle, which is about a quarter-inch wide, is a good substitute, or use fettuccine with this. The livers must be fresh!

2 tablespoons butter	1 tablespoon tomato paste
1 small onion, minced	1/2 cup dry white vermouth
2 garlic cloves, minced	1 large garlic clove
2 strips bacon, minced	3 tablespoons minced parsley
1/2 pound ground round	
1 1/2 teaspoons minced oregano or 1 teaspoon fresh dried	1 cup heavy cream
	4 quarts water
1 teaspoon salt	1 tablespoon salt
1/8 teaspoon pepper	1/2–2/3 pound pappardelle or other broad egg noodles
1/2 pound fresh chicken livers, cut into eighths	1 cup fresh-grated Parmesan

In a large skillet over medium heat, melt the butter. In it stir-fry the onion and garlic until the onion is translucent—5 to 6 minutes. Stir in the bacon pieces and cook, stirring, for 5 minutes. Stir in the ground beef and sauté until it is browning—another 5 minutes. Season with oregano, salt, and pepper and stir in the chicken livers. Simmer 2 or 3 minutes more, stirring, then stir in the tomato paste combined with the vermouth and cook for 3 minutes. Crush the garlic into the sauce and stir in the parsley. Cook 1 minute more. Stir in the cream, cook 30 seconds, and turn off the heat.

While the sauce is cooking, bring the water and salt to a rapid boil in a large covered kettle over high heat, and in it cook the noodles, uncovered, until barely tender. Drain.

Bring the sauce to simmering and scrape into a warm serving dish. At once toss the noodles in the sauce, and serve with fresh-grated Parmesan.

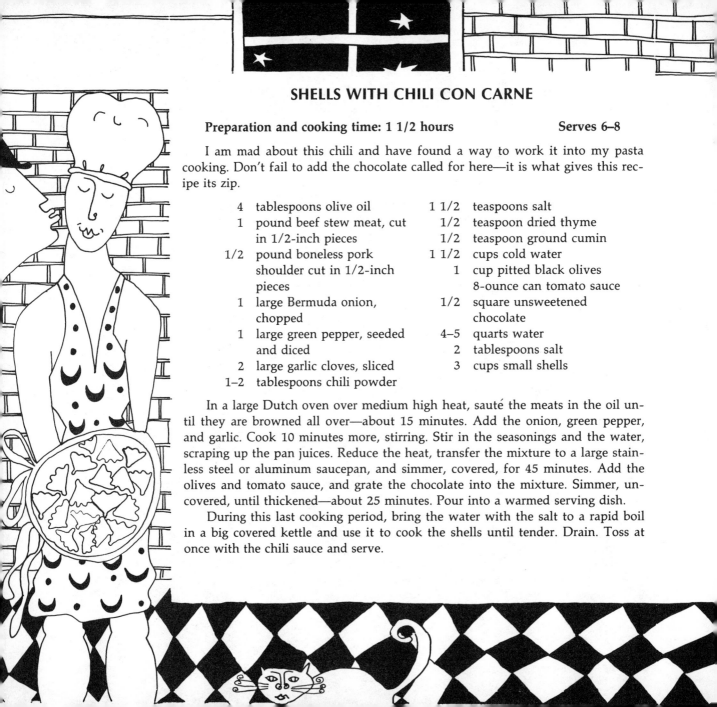

SHELLS WITH CHILI CON CARNE

Preparation and cooking time: 1 1/2 hours   **Serves 6–8**

I am mad about this chili and have found a way to work it into my pasta cooking. Don't fail to add the chocolate called for here—it is what gives this recipe its zip.

4	tablespoons olive oil	1 1/2	teaspoons salt
1	pound beef stew meat, cut in 1/2-inch pieces	1/2	teaspoon dried thyme
		1/2	teaspoon ground cumin
1/2	pound boneless pork shoulder cut in 1/2-inch pieces	1 1/2	cups cold water
		1	cup pitted black olives
1	large Bermuda onion, chopped		8-ounce can tomato sauce
		1/2	square unsweetened chocolate
1	large green pepper, seeded and diced	4–5	quarts water
2	large garlic cloves, sliced	2	tablespoons salt
1–2	tablespoons chili powder	3	cups small shells

In a large Dutch oven over medium high heat, sauté the meats in the oil until they are browned all over—about 15 minutes. Add the onion, green pepper, and garlic. Cook 10 minutes more, stirring. Stir in the seasonings and the water, scraping up the pan juices. Reduce the heat, transfer the mixture to a large stainless steel or aluminum saucepan, and simmer, covered, for 45 minutes. Add the olives and tomato sauce, and grate the chocolate into the mixture. Simmer, uncovered, until thickened—about 25 minutes. Pour into a warmed serving dish.

During this last cooking period, bring the water with the salt to a rapid boil in a big covered kettle and use it to cook the shells until tender. Drain. Toss at once with the chili sauce and serve.

FETTUCCINE CACCIATORE

Preparation and cooking time: 50–60 minutes   **Serves 4–6**

Cacciatore means "hunter." This is very rich!

1 1/2	pounds chicken thighs	4	tip sprigs each of basil, parsley, oregano, thyme
3	tablespoons olive oil		
1/2	medium Bermuda onion	1	small bay leaf
2	large cloves garlic	1	clove garlic
8	ounces mushrooms	1/2	teaspoon Pommery mustard
1/2	teaspoon salt		
1/4	teaspoon pepper	4–5	quarts water
	29-ounce can whole tomatoes in tomato puree	2	tablespoons salt
		2/3	pound fettuccine
1/2	cup dry wine	1	cup fresh-grated Parmesan cheese

With a small pointed knife, cut into the flesh of each chicken thigh to the bone; slice along the bone and free the meat. (Reserve the bones to make stock.) Cut flesh and skin into bite-size pieces.

In a large, heavy skillet over high heat, heat the oil and mince the onion and garlic into it. Stir and fry until the onions color a little—6 to 7 minutes—then stir in the chicken pieces and continue to sauté until browned—8 to 10 minutes. Reduce the heat if the onion is beginning to burn. Wipe the mushrooms and quarter them into the skillet. Season with salt and pepper, and stir in the tomatoes and puree with the wine. Scrape up the pan juices and turn the heat to low. Mince the herbs and crumble the bay leaf over the sauce. Cover the skillet and simmer for 15 to 20 minutes or until the sauce is very thick. Crush a garlic clove into the sauce and mix in the mustard.

Meanwhile, in a big covered kettle over high heat, bring the water with the salt to a rapid boil, and in it cook the fettuccine, uncovered, until just tender. Drain. Turn the cacciatore sauce into a warmed serving dish, pile the drained fettuccine on top, toss together, and serve at once. Offer fresh-grated Parmesan on the side, and pass the pepper mill.

SPAGHETTI WITH HAMBURGERS LAFAYETTE

Preparation and cooking time: 30–40 minutes   **Serves 4**

Hamburger Lafayette is ground round beef sautéed medium-rare with Snail Butter melting over it. We set it on a bed of pasta sauced with cheeses, butter, and eggs, and offer with it a salad flavored with fresh oregano. It makes a wonderful, hearty meal for family nights and pasta lovers.

1/4	recipe Snail Butter (p. 43)	2/3	cup grated Jarlsberg cheese
1	pound ground round	1/4	cup fresh-grated Parmesan cheese
4	quarts water		
2	tablespoons salt	2	egg yolks
1/2	pound spaghetti	1/2	cup heavy cream
1/2	stick butter		Salt

Prepare the Snail Butter and set to chill.

Cut the hamburger into thick slices. (Touch it as little as possible; compacting the meat makes it tough and dry.)

In a big covered kettle over high heat, bring the water and salt to a rapid boil. Cook the spaghetti in it, uncovered, until just tender. Drain.

Meanwhile, put the 1/2 stick of butter into a serving dish to warm, and prepare the cheeses and the yolks. Turn the just-drained spaghetti into the serving dish and toss with the melted butter. Sprinkle half of the Jarlsberg cheese over it and toss again. Sprinkle the Parmesan over the spaghetti and toss again. Combine the yolks with the cream, pour over the pasta, and toss well. Sprinkle with the reserved Jarlsberg cheese and set under the broiler on high until colored.

Put a heavy skillet over medium-high heat and sprinkle with salt. Heat to very hot, then put the hamburger patties into it and sauté for 3 minutes on one side, turn and sauté 1 minute more. Turn off the heat. Take the pasta from under the broiler, set the hamburgers on top, mash onto each hamburger a tablespoon of Snail Butter, and serve.

SNAIL BUTTER

Preparation time: 10 minutes   **Yield: 1/2 cup**

Snail Butter is the garlic-and-parsley mélange with which the big French snails are stuffed before baking. A quarter of the amount here is enough to top the hamburgers in the recipe on the opposite page, but make the lot and keep it in the fridge. It stores for weeks, and just a little on grilled meat creates miracles of flavor. It can save a lackluster pasta sauce, and makes heavenly Garlic Bread and stuffed mushrooms (see *Mad About Mushrooms*).

1 small bunch parsley	3 large garlic cloves
2 big green onions	1 stick soft butter

Rinse, stem, and air-dry the parsley. In a food processor, a blender, or in a bowl by hand, mince the parsley until really fine. Place it in a saucer, then measure 2 heaping packed tablespoons back into the processing bowl. Trim away 2 or 3 inches from the tops of the onions, peel off the outer skin, and mince the onions and the garlic with the parsley. Mince as fine as possible. Beat the butter into the herbs until well combined. The butter will be a beautiful pale green. Scrape into a small container that has a lid.

Cover, and store in the refrigerator. Use as needed.

Variation: Spaghetti with Snail Butter Sauce—Omit the hamburger in the Spaghetti with Hamburger Lafayette, and don't chill the Snail Butter after it is completed. Instead, place the Snail Butter in a warm serving dish just before you drain the cooked spaghetti, and toss the spaghetti with the Snail Butter until well coated. Omit the Jarlsberg Cheese and serve with 1 cup fresh-grated Parmesan cheese on the side, and pass the pepper mill. This is a very quick and easy sauce for spaghetti, and gloriously garlicky!

SALADS AND STARTERS

SALAD (AND) DRESSING MAISON

Preparation time: 5–8 minutes   **Yield: sauces 4 portions**

To dress salads for pasta meals, I use the best olive oil I can afford, beg, or borrow. I make a basic dressing in the salad bowl and season the salad again after it has been tossed with that dressing. The bowl is wooden and cone-shaped at the bottom, which makes it easy to mash the garlic and salt together—the beginning of any good salad dressing. I use wine vinegar—red for meat meals, white for fish meals and lighter foods. I often add lemon juice to salads for fish meals, mixing it half-and-half with white vinegar. To have salad dressing on hand for saucing a plate of antipasto, cold pasta salads, and such, I make a dressing as described here, using twice the amount of ingredients. Bottled and capped, it keeps almost indefinitely in the refrigerator if any is left over. Fresh oregano, thyme, rosemary, chervil, and particularly parsley and basil are herbs that enhance salads for pasta meals. If you can, grow your own—indoors in winter, outdoors in a window box in summer. No dried herb can do for a salad what a fresh herb can. To have crisp greens, clean, rinse, drain, and store them in a plastic bag in the crisper. Shake the water off before using the greens.

1	small garlic clove	2	teaspoons wine vinegar, and more
1/2	teaspoon salt		
	Grating pepper	2	teaspoons minced fresh herbs
1/4	teaspoon Pommery or Maille mustard	2–4	cups crisped greens (mache, lettuce, arugula, watercress, or others)
2	tablespoons olive oil, and more		

Peel and slice the garlic thin, put in a wooden salad bowl, sprinkle salt over it, and with the back of a round spoon, preferably wooden, mash them together to make a paste. Mix in the pepper and mustard, then whip in the oil, vinegar, and herbs. Pile the greens on top, and chill until ready to serve. Toss the greens with the dressing and herbs 28 times, taste, and add oil and vinegar by the teaspoonful and any other seasonings your taste dictates until the taste is right.

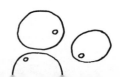

PANZANELLA AND PASTA SALAD

Preparation time: 15 minutes
Chilling time: 30 minutes or more

Serves 4–6

Panzanella is a way of making a tossed salad heartier by adding bread. I like it because in France we eat bread with everything. My father has been known to eat bread with dessert. (Scouts' honor!) And I also like it because this is a nifty way to use good baguettes gone stale. (The other way is in a nice broth.) Left-over cold pasta in salads can be very good. When cooking pasta with salad in mind, add double the amount of salt and 1 tablespoon of vegetable oil—don't waste expensive olive oil here. After the cooking water is drained, fill the kettle with cold running water. When the pasta has cooled, drain again. Use garden-ripened tomatoes. This salad is great with broiled meats, omelets, grilled fish.

1/4 stale crisp French or Italian bread	1/4 small Bermuda onion
3 tablespoons olive oil	1/3 green pepper
1 large garlic clove	1 large garden-ripe tomato
2 recipes Salad Dressing (p. 44, no greens)	1–2 cups cooked spaghettini, cut up (see p. 46)
4 flat anchovy fillets	1 tablespoon each minced parsley and basil

With a big sharp knife, cut the bread into bite-size cubes. Heat a big, heavy skillet over medium-high heat and warm the oil in it. Mince the garlic and add it. Sauté 1 minute, then add the stale bread pieces and stir and cook for 2 or 3 minutes, until all the oil is absorbed.

Prepare the Salad Dressing Maison but mash anchovies into the garlic and omit salt. Sliver the onion, green pepper, and tomato and add the sauce and toss together. Add the bread, toss, and refrigerate for 30 minutes.

Before serving, add the cooked spaghettini, cut up. Toss well, and increase oil, vinegar, salt, and pepper to taste. Toss with the minced herbs.

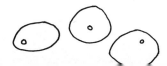

SPAGHETTINI SALAD PLATTER

Preparation time: 30 minutes
Chilling time: 30 minutes   Serves 4–6

I discovered this unusual and delicious cold pasta dish when I was making bread salad, Panzanella, page 45, and found I had cooked more spaghettini than I needed for another dish.

4–5	quarts water	5	anchovy fillets
4	tablespoons salt	12	large black Greek olives
1	tablespoon oil	4	tablespoons minced
1/2	pound spaghettini		parsley
2	recipes Salad Dressing	2	ripe tomatoes
	Maison (p. 44)	1	green pepper

In a big covered, kettle over high heat, bring the water with the salt and the oil to a rapid boil, and in it cook the spaghettini, uncovered, until barely tender. Drain, cover with cold running water until cooled, and drain again. Cut through the mass in the colander two or three times with a sharp knife to make the strands a little easier to handle.

Make the sauce for Salad Dressing Maison in a salad bowl, substituting the anchovy fillets for the salt in that recipe. Toss the drained spaghettini in the sauce. Slice the olives and add to the bowl. Taste and add more salt and pepper as needed. Toss again, and chill for 30 minutes. Sprinkle the parsley over the spaghettini mixture, toss several times, then turn out onto a bed of two cups of crisped salad greens such as Boston, Bibb, or romaine lettuce. Cut the tomatoes and peppers into rounds and strips and garnish the platter.

Variation: Spaghettini Salad with Swordfish—wonderful with cooked, cut-up chunks of swordfish, about 1/2 pound. Mince 2 green onions over the salad before tossing, and omit the tomatoes and peppers.

MACARONI AND CHEESE SALAD

Preparation time: 15–20 minutes
Chilling time: 30 minutes or more   Serves 6–8

Nifty for picnics, this classic recipe always pleases guests, and children love it. This is especially pretty on a bed of spinach leaves or golden-green escarole. It's grand Fourth of July fare served with hamburgers, cold ham, hot dogs.

4–5	quarts water	1/2	cup minced celery
4	tablespoons salt	1	cup mild cheddar cheese, cubed
1	tablespoon oil		
3	cups elbow macaroni	1/2	cup mayonnaise
1	tablespoon grated onion	3	tablespoons sour cream
3	tablespoons minced green pepper	1	teaspoon Pommery or Maille mustard
3	tablespoons minced pimiento		Salt and pepper
		4	cups crisped greens

In a big covered kettle over high heat, bring the water with the salt and the oil to a rapid boil and in it cook the macaroni, uncovered, until just tender. Drain, cover with cold water, and drain again.

Put the macaroni in a large salad bowl and sprinkle over it the onion, pepper, pimiento, celery, and cheddar cheese. In a small bowl, mix together the mayonnaise, sour cream, and mustard, pour over the macaroni mixture, and toss everything together. Taste, and add salt and pepper as needed. Chill, covered, for 30 minutes, then turn out onto a bed of crisped greens.

GREEK SALAD WITH FETA CHEESE

Preparation time: 30 minutes
Chilling time: 30 minutes or more   Serves 4

Cheese salads are heaven with pasta meals, and great starters! Feta (sheep's) cheese is a gift from Greece—tart and salty, and excellent with ripe black olives, tomatoes, and garden vegetables. Don't limit yourself to the vegetables described here. Let your garden, your own taste, or the salad bar at the supermarket or greengrocer be your guide. Yummm!

1	small garlic clove	1/4	small zucchini
1/2	teaspoon salt	1/2	green pepper
1/8	teaspoon pepper	15	cherry tomatoes
1/4	teaspoon Pommery mustard	6–8	big mushrooms
3	tablespoons olive oil	10	jumbo ripe pitted olives or black Greek olives
1	tablespoon lemon juice	4	tip sprigs fresh thyme
1/4	Bermuda onion	8	ounces feta cheese
1/2	cup cauliflower florets	1/4	cup packed spinach leaves
12–14	snow peas, stemmed		

Slice the garlic, place in a wooden salad bowl, sprinkle the salt over it, and with the back of a wooden spoon, mash the salt and garlic together to make a paste. Stir in the pepper and mustard, then the olive oil, and beat in the lemon juice. Sliver the onion and vegetables and sprinkle over the dressing; halve the cherry tomatoes and add. Slice the mushrooms into thin T shapes, quarter the olives, and add. Mince the thyme and sprinkle over all. Dice the feta cheese, and add, then toss the salad five or six times. Cover with spinach leaves and chill for 30 minutes or until ready to serve. Toss again before serving. Taste, and add oil, vinegar, and seasonings if needed.

Variation: Add a cup or two of cooked cold pasta to this if you wish, and increase the salad dressing ingredients to suit your taste.

TOMATO-BRIE SALAD PLATTER

Preparation time: 20 minutes   **Serves 4**

Among the great things in life are tomatoes, ripe from the garden, sauced with fresh basil and garlic. Here is a nifty salad platter combining these elements and Brie cheese, perfect as a starter course, as a luncheon main course, or as a side plate with a pasta dish. Brie from Meaux is imported from France, and seems to me richer than the others.

3	large ripe tomatoes	1	tablespoon oil
1/3–1/2	pound Brie	1	teaspoon wine vinegar
1	recipe Salad Dressing	10	tip sprigs basil, or large
	Maison (p. 44), no greens,		leaves
	no herbs		Basil sprigs
1	large garlic clove		

Remove the stem cores from the tomatoes. Discard the end pieces. Slice the tomatoes into 12 thick rounds. Cut the Brie wedge into 12 strips about 1/2 to 1 inch wide. Prepare the salad dressing, adding 1 large garlic clove, 1 tablespoon of oil, and 1 teaspoon of vinegar from the list of ingredients here to the recipe on page 44. Omit the 2 teaspoons of herbs in that recipe. Scrape this dressing into a blender or a food processor, add 10 fresh basil tip sprigs, and process long enough to mince the basil. Arrange the tomato slices on a serving platter, and set a piece of Brie on each slice. Pour the Salad Dressing over the tomato and Brie. Garnish with sprigs of basil, and chill if possible, before serving.

Variation: Tomato-Goat Cheese Salad Platter—I love the salty taste of goat cheese, and its stark whiteness on a salad platter. A wonderful combination with ripe tomatoes—handle as above, but for the dressing use minced fresh parsley combined with minced fresh thyme instead of basil.

SHELLS AND TUNA WITH FRESH HERBS

Preparation time: 30 minutes
Chilling time: 30 minutes or more   Serves 6–8

This is especially pretty when the pink tuna and the herbs are served in a white dish or a glass bowl. It's a nifty luncheon or a perfect starter salad. Offer garlic bread as an accompaniment, page 57.

4–5 quarts boiling water	4 teaspoons capers
4 tablespoons salt	1/4 pound greek olives, sliced
1 tablespoon oil	8–10 large basil leaves
6 ounces small shells (1/2 package)	6 each large parsley and thyme tip sprigs
2 large garlic cloves, sliced	6-ounce can chunk light tuna in oil
1 1/2 teaspoons salt	16-ounce can tiny peas, drained
5 tablespoons olive oil	Crisped salad greens
2 tablespoons white wine vinegar	
1/2 small Bermuda onion, minced	

In a big covered kettle over high heat, bring the water with the salt and the oil to a rapid boil. In it cook the shells, uncovered until tender. Drain. Cover with cold water.

Meanwhile, in a wooden bowl with the tip of a wooden spoon, mash the garlic with the salt to make a paste. Stir in the oil and vinegar, onion, capers, and olives. Mince the herbs into the dressing. (I roll the basil leaves up into a stick and then cut them over the bowl with a small sharp knife.) Mix well, then drop the drained tuna into this, and break the tuna into small pieces. Toss the peas with the mixture. Drain the shells well. Add to the salad and toss thoroughly. Place the salad on a serving platter covered with crisp greens. Cover and chill for 30 minutes before serving.

CHICKEN AND TORTIGLIONI PLATTER

Preparation time: 1 hour   **Serves 4**

Tortiglioni is a corkscrew pasta, but almost any other pasta will work well in this platter served at room temperature.

4–5 quarts water	8 ounces mushrooms
2 tablespoons salt	1/2 cup broccoli florets
1 small bay leaf	salt and pepper
1/2 teaspoon dried thyme	1 bunch green onions, trimmed
8 chicken thighs or 4 legs	1 tablespoon Pesto Sauce (p. 13) or minced basil
2 cups tortiglioni	
3 tablespoons olive oil	
2 large cloves garlic	

In a big covered kettle over high heat, bring the water with the salt, bay leaf, and thyme to a rapid boil. Put the chicken into it, reduce the heat, cover, and simmer for 45 minutes. Lift the chicken out, cool, discard the bones and skin, and cut into bite-size pieces. Bring the broth back to a boil, and in it cook the tortiglioni until just tender. Drain and reserve the broth.

Meanwhile, in an electric frying pan or a big, heavy skillet, warm the oil over medium heat and mince the garlic into it. Wipe the mushrooms. Remove the tough end of the stems and slice the mushrooms. Add to the oil and cook 2 or 3 minutes. Stir in the broccoli florets and sauté 2 minutes more. Season with salt and pepper. Lift the vegetables into a serving dish. Slice the onions 1/4-inch thick, add to the skillet, and stir and fry for 2 minutes, then scrape them over the vegetables. Add the cut-up chicken to the skillet, pour over it 1/4 cup of broth, and stir in the Pesto Sauce or minced basil. Heat through, and place on the serving dish. Pile the drained tortiglioni over the chicken, and toss everything together several times. Serve at room temperature or slightly cooled.

RIGATONI SALAD PRIMAVERA

Preparation time: 60 minutes
Chilling time: 30 minutes   **Serves 4**

This is best made from tiny spring vegetables—sliver-thin baby green beans, young carrots, florets of young broccoli, skinny asparagus stalks, tender snowpeas, baby zucchini. In the city, I buy vegetables in half-cup lots from the greengrocer who sells ready-to-use salad vegetables. This recipe calls for rigatoni, but shells or another substantial pasta will do. A nice salad for cookouts and take-along parties.

1/2	loosely packed cup of each of 4 green vegetables, cut matchstick thin	1	recipe Salad Dressing Maison (p. 44), no greens
1/2	cup carrot rounds	4	thin green onions, trimmed
3	tablespoons good olive oil or butter	2–3	cups rigatoni or ziti
1	large clove garlic	4–5	quarts water
1	teaspoon salt	4	tablespoons salt
1/3	teaspoon sugar	1	tablespoon oil
		1/3	cup minced parsley

Prepare the vegetables and arrange them near an electric frying pan set at 400°, or a big skillet over high heat. Heat the oil, slice the garlic into it, then, one lot at a time starting with beans and carrots, stir in the vegetables and sauté for a few seconds before adding the next batch. Season with salt and sugar, and stir and fry for about 5 minutes. Turn off the heat. Cover the skillet.

In a salad bowl, prepare the salad dressing as directed but increase the mustard to 1/2 teaspoon. Slice the onions into the dressing.

In a big covered kettle, bring the water to a rapid boil with the salt and the oil and cook the rigatoni or ziti in it, uncovered, until tender. Drain. Cool in cold water; drain. Toss with the salad dressing until well coated. Pile the cooked vegetables and their juices on top of the pasta and toss together. Chill for 30 minutes. Sprinkle with parsley, and serve.

TORTIGLIONI VINAIGRETTE WITH ARTICHOKES

Preparation time: 30–40 minutes
Chilling time: 30 minutes or more

Serves 4–6

Tortiglioni are those pretty twists that are ideal for picking up a rich sauce! This makes a great-looking party plate especially when served in tomato cups as on our front cover. Serve with crusty bread and butter as a first course. In addition to the ingredients here, you will need the 2 cups of crisped greens called for in the recipe for Salad Dressing Maison.

4–5	quarts water	1	teaspoon fresh minced tarragon or 1/2 teaspoon dried
4	tablespoons salt		
1	tablespoon oil		
2	cups tortiglioni	6	ounces mushrooms
	9-ounce package frozen artichoke hearts	1	small ripe tomato
		4	green onions, trimmed
2	recipes Salad Dressing Maison (p. 44) and greens	8	thin slices cucumber, rind on
		1	tablespoon minced parsley

In a big covered kettle over high heat, bring the water with the salt and the oil to a rapid boil, and cook the tortiglioni in it, uncovered, until tender. Drain, and cover with cold water.

Cook the artichokes, and meanwhile prepare the sauce for Salad Dressing Maison and stir the tarragon into it. Remove the tough stem ends from the mushrooms and quarter the mushrooms. Put the warm, drained artichokes into the dressing along with the mushrooms. Toss together. Drain the tortiglioni, add to the bowl, and toss well. Add the tomato sliced into thin wedges, the green onions, minced, and refrigerate about 30 minutes.

Just before serving, spread 2 cups of spinach or a combination of crisped greens over a serving platter. Toss the salad several times, season to your taste, and scrape over the greens. Garnish with cucumber slices and sprinkle minced parsley over all.

THE PASTA DINNER

ANTIPASTO PLATTER

Preparation time: 30 minutes   **Serves 4**

An elegant pasta dinner deserves music and flowers—classical guitar, the liquid voice of Mediterranean nights—geraniums and spicy carnations in a centerpiece of fruits and vegetables such as artichokes and asparagus. And a superb antipasto platter. Anything can become an antipasto, from sardines smothered in parsley minced with Bermuda onions to fragrant, ripe cantaloupe chunks wrapped in prosciutto, the thin elegantly flavored Italian ham. Leftover cooked vegetables of every sort (particularly cooked beans, dried or snap), marinated in Salad Dressing Maison with minced green onions and parsley, make good antipasti, as do leftover meats and seafoods in the same sauce made piquant with mustard and green herbs. The salads and salad plates in the preceding section make wonderful antipasti for meals that might be followed by a meat course like the Veal Scaloppine, pages 58–59, or meaty Baked Eggplant Parmesan, page 60. The Antipasto Platter here includes the elements you are most likely to find ready at the grocery store. Add others of your own devising—chunks of cheese, canned seafoods, paté, cooked pork products and sausages, baby vegetables from the garden. Serve plenty of crispy bread and butter with the Antipasto Platter. Heat the loaf in its paper wrapper for 10 to 15 minutes at 375°, and bring to the table warm. (Note: You can tell a ripe cantaloupe by its melon fragrance: Sniff before you buy!)

1	recipe Salad Dressing Maison (p. 44), and greens	12	jumbo black olives, unpitted
1	green onion, trimmed and minced	8	cherry tomatoes
1/2	ripe cantaloupe	4–8	sardines, drained
1/4	pound prosciutto	1	teaspoon capers
2	hard-boiled eggs, shelled	8	slices garlic sausage, very thin
4	anchovies	1/4	pound goat or feta cheese
12	artichoke hearts in oil		

Prepare the Salad Dressing Maison, and mince into it the green onion and the herbs from the Salad Dressing recipe. On a serving platter, set out 2 cups of crisped greens, including, if possible, a few leaves of arugula or mache. On the greens, arrange bite-size chunks of the cantaloupe wrapped in prosciutto; the hard-boiled eggs, halved, topped by curled-up anchovies; the artichoke hearts, drained; olives, tomatoes, sardines topped by capers. Fold the sausage slices in four and tuck them in among the ingredients. Set rounds of goat or cubes of feta cheese decoratively over the platter. Sprinkle with salad dressing, and chill for 30 minutes or more before serving.

RAW VEGETABLES WITH BAGNA CAUDA

Preparation time: 30 minutes   **Serves 8–10**

This is a wonderful hot dip appetizer to take the place of antipasti when you are planning a stand-up buffet or dinner. The time involved is very brief if you can find prepared, cut-up raw vegetables at the local supermarket. If you prepare the vegetables yourself, this recipe will take another 30 or 40 minutes. Use quartered mushrooms; florets of cauliflower and broccoli; rounds of zucchini and summer squash; carrot sticks, celery, fennel, and the garden produce. *Bagna Cauda* means "hot bath" in Italian.

8	cups raw vegetables and greens
6	large garlic cloves, sliced
12	anchovy fillets in oil, drained

2	sticks butter
1	cup olive oil
	Salt and pepper

Chill the vegetables and arrange them on a large platter.

In a small fondue dish, mash together the garlic and anchovies, and set over low heat. Stir until the mixture thickens. A little at a time, stir in the butter, then the oil. Taste, and add salt or pepper if needed. Set over a small fondue heating element, an alcohol lamp, or a Sterno container and keep warm, but do not keep so hot that the sauce continues to cook. Serve with the raw vegetables as a dip.

EGG DROP SOUP WITH SPINACH

Preparation and cooking time: 30 minutes   **Serves 4**

This is a delicious version of Stracciatella, a Roman specialty—it's creamy, carries a hint of garlic, basil, and lemon, and makes a wonderful first course for a pasta dinner. A favorite!

1/2 pound fresh spinach	3 tablespoons fresh-grated Parmesan cheese
1 garlic clove	
2 cups chicken bouillon	2 tablespoons fresh-grated Swiss cheese, such as Jarlsberg
2 cups bottled clam juice or 2 more cups chicken bouillon	
	3 medium basil leaves
1/2 teaspoon grated lemon rind	1 tablespoon sweet butter
3 large eggs	1/2 teaspoon grated lemon rind
	1 small garlic clove

Measure, prepare, and line up all the ingredients before you begin. Pick the leaves from the spinach stems; discard the stems. Wash the leaves seven or eight times in cold water, lifting them from the water to the colander at each change of water until no sand remains in the washing bowl. Put the spinach into a heavy saucepan with only the water clinging to the leaves, and slice the garlic clove over it. Cover tight. Cook over high heat until the spinach has wilted completely—2 or 3 minutes. Remove the cover and boil until all the water is gone—another few seconds—then turn off the heat and chop the spinach a little with 2 knives.

Meanwhile, over high heat in a large saucepan, bring the broth(s) to boiling with the grated lemon rind. Turn off the heat. While this is going on, break the eggs into a large bowl and, with an electric beater on high, beat them for 2 minutes, then beat in the two cheeses.

When you are ready to serve the soup, bring the broth back to boiling, turn the heat to low, and beat about a third of the broth in a thin stream into the eggs, then put the broth saucepan back over low heat and whisk the egg mixture into it. *Do not let it boil*—bring the soup to barely simmering, then turn off the heat. Mince the basil leaves into the soup, stir in the butter and the lemon rind. Crush the garlic into the broth, stir in the spinach, and serve. Pass the pepper mill.

GARLIC BREAD WITH FRESH HERBS

Preparation time: 15 minutes
Baking time: 10–12 minutes   **Serves 4–6**

Crispy golden bread hot from the oven and redolent of garlic and fresh herbs is one of the great aromas of this world. And it is one of the easiest treats to prepare. Buy the best loaf of French or Italian bread you can find. Use it fresh. (But know that this recipe is quite good made from a slightly stale loaf or from one that has been frozen.) Snail Butter has lots of herbs: a simpler recipe is to beat 1 stick of butter with 3 large cloves of garlic for every 18-inch loaf of slender French or Italian bread, and proceed as here.

1   18-inch loaf French or
    Italian bread
1   recipe soft Snail Butter
    (p. 43)

Heat the oven to 400°. Prepare the Snail Butter. Lay out a 24-inch strip of foil and place the loaf in the middle of it. With a bread knife, cut diagonal slices into the bread, but do not cut all the way through—cut just as far as the bottom crust (if you cut through, never mind, but make sure the paper has not been cut, or the loaf may leak while baking). With a broad butter knife, generously smear each side of each slice with Snail Butter, then press the slices back together. Close the foil around the loaf.

Bake in the preheated oven for 10 minutes, then open the foil and bake for another 10 or until all the butter has melted and the loaf crisped. Lift the foil into a long bread basket and serve in the foil, or break slices into a round basket lined with two paper napkins. Serve hot.

VEAL SCALOPPINE WITH LEMON

Preparation time: 10–15 minutes
Cooking time: 2–5 minutes   **Serves 4**

Scaloppine are thin (quarter-inch) slices from the top round of a young cow or calf. Pounded thin by the butcher or by you, they are twice their original size when ready to cook, take only a couple of minutes to sauté to tenderness, and are the perfect meat accompaniment for a great pasta—Fettuccine in Salsa Bianca or Spaghetti with Fresh Tomato Sauce. In a continental home, the scaloppine would be served after the pasta course, but I serve them with the pasta, usually on the same dinner plate. Sometimes (for more formal meals) I serve the meat alone on a dinner plate with lots of parsley garnish, with the pasta on the side in a pasta dish. I follow this with a simple salad of tossed greens dressed with Salad Dressing Maison (p. 44), and add a few leaves of arugula, a sour Italian green. (It has a taste of its own that I am mad about.)

If you are serving a pasta course with scaloppine, have the scaloppine ready to cook before you begin the pasta sauce, especially if it is one of the fast-moving sauces.

4	scaloppine (about 1/4 pound)	2	tablespoons lemon juice
1/4	teaspoon salt	2	tablespoons butter
1/3	cup all-purpose flour	2	tablespoons minced parsley
1	tablespoon vegetable oil	4	thin round lemons, seeded
2	tablespoons butter	1/4	bunch parsley

On a wooden board with a wooden mallet, pound the scaloppine, working to stretch them as thin and as large as possible—1/4 inch thick when finished. Salt each piece. Spread the flour in a large plate, lay the scaloppine in it, and turn, flouring both sides well.

Heat a large heavy skillet over medium-high heat. Add the oil and melt the butter in it. When the froth dies down and the butter begins to color a bit, slide the scaloppine into it, piece by piece, moving each around so it doesn't stick. Cook for 1 to 2 minutes, until browned. Turn and repeat.

Remove the skillet from the heat. Lift the scaloppine to a warm serving plate or dinner plates. Stir the lemon juice into the skillet, scraping up the juices stuck to the bottom. Return to the heat and stir in the butter, then the parsley, and cook 1 minute more. At once, scrape over the meat. Garnish each piece of meat with 1 lemon round and some parsley.

Variation: Veal Scaloppine with Marsala Sauce—Instead of lemon juice, this recipe flavors the scaloppine with Marsala, an Italian "cooked" wine with a rich flavor. Prepare and cook the scaloppine as in the basic recipe and transfer them to a warmed serving dish. To the skillet, add 1/2 cup dry Marsala, scraping up the pan juices. Return the skillet to the heat and stir over medium-high heat until the wine boils—about 30 seconds—then cook 5 minutes more. Stir the 2 tablespoons butter into the sauce, and as soon as it has melted, scrape the sauce over the scaloppine and serve.

ZUCCHINI SAUTÉ

Preparation and cooking time: 15–20 minutes　　　　**Serves 4**

I love briefly stir-fried zucchini with pasta meals.

1 tablespoon olive oil	Salt and pepper
1 large garlic clove, minced	1 teaspoon minced basil or
2 small, firm zucchini, stemmed and sliced thin (unpeeled)	parsley

Heat a wok, an electric fry pan, or a big heavy saucepan over medium-high heat, and warm the oil in it. Add the garlic; stir as it browns briefly, then add the zucchini and shake the wok or pan often so the pieces are constantly moving over the heated surface. Cook this way for about 3 minutes, then turn off the heat and let the vegetables finish tenderizing in their own heat until ready to serve. Taste and season with salt and pepper, if desired. Garnish with minced basil or parsley.

BAKED EGGPLANT PARMESAN

Preparation and baking time: 1 1/2 hours   **Serves 4–6**

This is a wonderfully "meaty" dish, nifty when vegetarians are coming to a pasta dinner. Serve your favorite simple pasta with it, and a salad.

2	medium eggplants, peeled		1	large garlic clove
	Salt		1/2	teaspoon oregano
1/2	cup all-purpose flour		1/3	cup minced parsley
1/8	teaspoon pepper			salt and pepper
1/2–3/4	cup olive oil		8	ounces ricotta cheese
2	medium onions, peeled		1/2	cup fresh-grated Parmesan cheese
4	ripe medium tomatoes, peeled, or 16-ounce can whole tomatoes, chopped		1/4	pound mozzarella cheese, sliced thin

Slice each eggplant into 4 or 6 slices, lengthwise. Salt lightly on all sides, pile one piece on another, then put a plate on top and a weight on the plate. (My mother used to use an old, heavy iron.) Allow 30 minutes to 1 hour for the eggplants to render their juice. Rinse and drain the pieces and pat really dry with paper towel. Dust with flour mixed with pepper.

In a large skillet over medium heat, heat the oil and fry the eggplant slices in it until they are lightly browned on each side—3 to 5 minutes. Lift the slices out of the oil, and reserve. Slice the onions, add them to the oil, stir in the tomatoes and their juices, mince the garlic and add to the skillet, stir in the oregano and the parsley. Simmer until the sauce thickens a little. Taste and add salt and pepper if desired. Turn off the heat.

Heat the oven to 450°. Meanwhile pour a third of the sauce into a shallow baking dish. Lay half the eggplant slices in the sauce, then spoon half the ricotta cheese over the eggplant slices and sprinkle with half the Parmesan. Repeat the layers and top with remaining sauce. Bake for 40 minutes. Place the mozzarella slices over the top of the dish and melt in the oven. Serve hot.

CHOCOLATE PASTA, BRANDY AND CREAM

Preparation and cooking time: 15–20 minutes   Serves 4

Yes, pasta for dessert: our back cover shows it in a tall glass. In New York, chocolate pasta is sold, fresh made by De Laurentiis, 15 Columbus Circle. Puddingy, rich, delicious—and a great conversation piece!

2/3	cup golden raisins	1	teaspoon salt
1/2	cup brandy	1/2–2/3	pound, chocolate
6	ounces milk chocolate		fettuccine
4–5	quarts water	1	cup sweet whipped cream

In a medium mixing bowl, combine the raisins, brandy, and chocolate, broken into small pieces. In a big covered kettle over high heat, bring the water with the salt to a rapid boil and in it cook the fettuccine, uncovered, until barely tender. Drain. At once toss with the ingredients in the mixing bowl, until the chocolate is all completely melted. Divide the pasta among 4 tall, stemmed glasses. Allow to cool. Before serving, garnish with cream.

ZABAGLIONE

Preparation and cooking time: 20–30 minutes   Serves 6–8

For me, this is *the* Italian dessert—light and lovely.

5	large egg yolks	1/2	cup dry Marsala
5	heaping tablespoons	1	cup sweet whipped cream
	Sugar		

Put 3 or 4 cups of water to boil in a large kettle over high heat. In a large crockery bowl with an electric beater, beat the yolks until thick and lemon colored, then, a tablespoon at a time, beat in the sugar. Place over the boiling water, reduce the heat to low, and continue to beat, adding the Marsala little by little. When the mixture mounds, spoon into tall dessert goblets, and serve at once with whipped cream.

RUM CAKE

Preparation and baking time: 40 minutes
Chilling time: 4 hours or more

Serves 8

A light, spongy cake perfect with Café Espresso, or with finger fruits, or sherbet. Add as much of the rum sauce as you like—the alcohol cooks out, so it's OK for everyone. Especially pretty baked in a fluted tube pan.

4 large eggs	1/2 cup water
Hot water	1/4 cup sugar
1 1/2 cups sifted cake flour	1/2 cup dark rum
3/4 cup sugar	2 tablespoons frozen orange juice concentrate
1 tablespoon baking powder	
Pinch of salt	1/4 cup pecans, chopped
1/4 cup melted butter	2 tablespoons grated orange rind
1 1/2 teaspoons grated lemon rind	1 cup sweet whipped cream (optional)
Soft butter, flour	

Heat the oven to 350°. Put the eggs into a large bowl with hot water.

Into a large mixing bowl sift together the flour, sugar, baking powder, and salt. Remove and dry the eggs. Discard the water. Break the eggs into the bowl they were in and with an electric beater, beat until thick and lemon colored. With a whisk beat the eggs into the flour mixture, then beat in the butter and rind. Very generously butter a 6-cup tube pan, including the tube, then flour it and turn the batter into it. Smooth down the batter, making sure air pockets are removed. Bake 25 minutes at 350°. Check for doneness: Press on the cake top, and if it bounces back it is done. If not, bake another 5 minutes. Remove to a cake rack and cook 10 minutes. Over a serving dish deep enough to hold the sauce, set the pan upside down resting on the tube—it will cool and the cake will drop.

Meanwhile, over high heat bring to a rapid boil the water with the sugar. At once pour the rum into the boiling syrup, allow to come back to a boil, and turn off the heat. Stir in the orange juice concentrate, turn the sauce into a clean bowl, and chill to lukewarm in the freezer.

When the cake has dropped into the serving dish and is still warm, spoon tepid rum sauce over it until sauce sits unabsorbed in the saucer. Chill 4 hours if possible. Dust with chopped nuts, then with orange rind and, if you wish, garnish the sides of the dish with dollops of stiffly whipped sweetened cream.

CAFÉ ESPRESSO

Preparation time: 10 minutes   **Serves 4**

Espresso coffee is the grand finale to the pasta dinner—a brew so rich it rivals Turkish coffee and, like Turkish coffee, is served with sugar only, no cream. In America it is often served with a twist of lemon peel, so thin only the yellow (zest) is included. Cappuccino is espresso to which bubbling hot milk or light cream is added and topped with a dusting of cinnamon or nutmeg. There are home espresso machines available now with instructions for making espresso. More common is the French filtre type of coffee maker. With this system you boil the water in the bottom, steaming the ground coffee placed in the middle section, then turn the whole upside down to drip over the grounds. *Either will produce espresso only if the coffee used is French or Italian dark roast.* The best tasting coffee is made the European way, from just-ground beans. The proportions per cup for espresso are 6 tablespoons of boiling water to 2 level tablespoons of drip grind coffee. This also makes superb coffee from just-ground mocha and other coffee beans.

   1 2/3 cups boiling water
      8 level tablespoons *dark roast
         or espresso coffee*, ground fine

    4 twists lemon peel
      Sugar, cubes preferred

Make the coffee in whatever drip equipment you have, and serve in demitasse cups. Offer with it twists of lemon peel and sugar.

RECIPE LIST / INDEX